FOREWORD

The collection of "Everything Will Be Okay" travel phrasebooks published by T&P Books is designed for people traveling abroad for tourism and business. The phrasebooks contain what matters most - the essentials for basic communication. This is an indispensable set of phrases to "survive" while abroad.

This phrasebook will help you in most cases where you need to ask something, get directions, find out how much something costs, etc. It can also resolve difficult communication situations where gestures just won't help.

This book contains a lot of phrases that have been grouped according to the most relevant topics. The edition also includes a small vocabulary that contains roughly 3,000 of the most frequently used words. Another section of the phrasebook provides a gastronomical dictionary that may help you order food at a restaurant or buy groceries at the store.

Take "Everything Will Be Okay" phrasebook with you on the road and you'll have an irreplaceable traveling companion who will help you find your way out of any situation and teach you to not fear speaking with foreigners.

TABLE OF CONTENTS

Pronunciation	5
List of abbreviations	7
English-Arabic	9
Topical vocabulary	73
Gastronomic glossary	193

T&P Books Publishing

T&P Books Publishing

PHRASEBOOK

— ARABIC —

By Andrey Taranov

THE MOST IMPORTANT PHRASES

This phrasebook contains the most important phrases and questions for basic communication
Everything you need to survive overseas

T&P BOOKS

Phrasebook + 3000-word dictionary

English-Arabic phrasebook & topical vocabulary

By Andrey Taranov

The collection of "Everything Will Be Okay" travel phrasebooks published by T&P Books is designed for people traveling abroad for tourism and business. The phrasebooks contain what matters most - the essentials for basic communication. This is an indispensable set of phrases to "survive" while abroad.

This book also includes a small topical vocabulary that contains roughly 3,000 of the most frequently used words. Another section of the phrasebook provides a gastronomical dictionary that may help you order food at a restaurant or buy groceries at the store.

T&P Books Publishing
www.tpbooks.com

ISBN: 978-1-78716-930-2

This book is also available in E-book formats.
Please visit www.tpbooks.com or the major online bookstores.

PRONUNCIATION

T&P phonetic alphabet	Arabic example	English example
[a]	طفّى [ṭaffa]	shorter than in ask
[â]	إختار [iχtār]	calf, palm
[e]	هامبورجر [hamburger]	elm, medal
[i]	زفاف [zifâf]	shorter than in feet
[ī]	أبريل [abrīl]	feet, meter
[u]	كلكتا [kalkutta]	book
[ū]	جاموس [ʒâmūs]	fuel, tuna
[b]	بداية [bidāya]	baby, book
[d]	سعادة [saʿāda]	day, doctor
[ḍ]	وضع [waḍʿ]	[d] pharyngeal
[ʒ]	الأرجنتين [arʒantīn]	forge, pleasure
[ð]	تذكار [tiðkār]	pharyngealized th
[ẓ]	ظهر [ẓahar]	[z] pharyngeal
[f]	خفيف [χafīf]	face, food
[g]	جولف [gūlf]	game, gold
[h]	إتّجاه [ittiʒāh]	home, have
[ḥ]	أحبّ [aḥabb]	[h] pharyngeal
[y]	ذهبيّ [ðahabiy]	yes, New York
[k]	كرسيّ [kursiy]	clock, kiss
[l]	لمح [lamaḥ]	lace, people
[m]	مرصد [marṣad]	magic, milk
[n]	جنوب [ʒanūb]	sang, thing
[p]	كابتشينو [kaputʃīnu]	pencil, private
[q]	وثق [waθiq]	king, club
[r]	روح [rūḥ]	rice, radio
[s]	سخريّة [suχriyya]	city, boss
[ṣ]	معصم [miʿṣam]	[s] pharyngeal
[ʃ]	عشاء [ʿaʃāʾ]	machine, shark
[t]	تنّوب [tannūb]	tourist, trip
[ṭ]	خريطة [χarīṭa]	[t] pharyngeal
[θ]	ماموث [mamūθ]	month, tooth
[v]	فينتام [vitnām]	very, river
[w]	ودّع [waddaʿ]	vase, winter
[χ]	بخيل [baχīl]	as in Scots 'loch'
[ɣ]	تغدّى [taɣadda]	between [g] and [h]
[z]	ماعز [mâʿiz]	zebra, please

T&P phonetic alphabet	Arabic example	English example
['] (ayn)	[sab'a] سبعة	voiced pharyngeal fricative
['] (hamza)	[sa'al] سأل	glottal stop

LIST OF ABBREVIATIONS

Arabic abbreviations

du	-	plural noun (double)
f	-	feminine noun
m	-	masculine noun
pl	-	plural

English abbreviations

ab.	-	about
adj	-	adjective
adv	-	adverb
anim.	-	animate
as adj	-	attributive noun used as adjective
e.g.	-	for example
etc.	-	et cetera
fam.	-	familiar
fem.	-	feminine
form.	-	formal
inanim.	-	inanimate
masc.	-	masculine
math	-	mathematics
mil.	-	military
n	-	noun
pl	-	plural
pron.	-	pronoun
sb	-	somebody
sing.	-	singular
sth	-	something
v aux	-	auxiliary verb
vi	-	intransitive verb
vi, vt	-	intransitive, transitive verb
vt	-	transitive verb

T&P BOOKS

ARABIC
PHRASEBOOK

This section contains
important phrases that may
come in handy in various
real-life situations.
The phrasebook will help
you ask for directions, clarify
a price, buy tickets, and
order food at a restaurant

T&P Books Publishing

PHRASEBOOK
CONTENTS

The bare minimum	12
Questions	15
Needs	16
Asking for directions	18
Signs	20
Transportation. General phrases	22
Buying tickets	24
Bus	26
Train	28
On the train. Dialogue (No ticket)	29
Taxi	30
Hotel	32
Restaurant	35
Shopping	37
In town	39
Money	41

Time	43
Greetings. Introductions	45
Farewells	47
Foreign language	49
Apologies	50
Agreement	51
Refusal. Expressing doubt	52
Expressing gratitude	54
Congratulations. Best wishes	55
Socializing	56
Sharing impressions. Emotions	59
Problems. Accidents	61
Health problems	64
At the pharmacy	67
The bare minimum	69

T&P Books Publishing

The bare minimum

Excuse me, ...	ba'd ezznak, ... بعد إذنك، ...
Hello.	ahlan أهلاً
Thank you.	ʃokran شكراً
Good bye.	ella alliqā' إلى اللقاء
Yes.	aywā أيوة
No.	la'a لأ
I don't know.	ma'raʃʃ ما أعرفش
Where? | Where to? | When?	feyn? | lefeyn? | emta? إمتى؟ | لفين؟ | فين؟

I need ...	meḥtāg ... محتاج ...
I want ...	'āyez ... عايز ...
Do you have ...?	ya tara 'andak ...? يا ترى عندك... ؟
Is there a ... here?	feyh hena ...? فيه هنا ...؟
May I ...?	momken ...? ممكن ...؟
..., please (polite request)	... men faḍlak من فضلك ...

I'm looking for ...	ana badawwar 'la ... أنا بادور على ...
restroom	ḥammām حمام
ATM	makīnet ṣarraf 'āaly ماكينة صراف آلي
pharmacy (drugstore)	ṣaydaliya صيدلية
hospital	mostaʃfa مستشفى
police station	'essm el ʃorṭa قسم شرطة
subway	metro el anfā' مترو الأنفاق

taxi	taksi تاكسي
train station	mahattet el 'attr محطة القطر

My name is ...	essmy ... إسمي...
What's your name?	essmak eyh? اسمك إيه؟
Could you please help me?	te'ddar tesā'dny? تقدر تساعدني؟
I've got a problem.	ana 'andy moʃkela أنا عندي مشكلة
I don't feel well.	ana ta'bān أنا تعبان
Call an ambulance!	otlob 'arabeyet es'āf! أطلب عربية إسعاف!
May I make a call?	momken a'mel mokalma telefoniya? ممكن أعمل مكالمة تليفونية؟

I'm sorry.	ana 'āssif أنا آسف
You're welcome.	el 'afw العفو

I, me	ana أنا
you (inform.)	enta أنت
he	howwa هو
she	hiya هي
they (masc.)	homm هم
they (fem.)	homm هم
we	ehna احنا
you (pl)	entom انتم
you (sg, form.)	haddretak حضرتك

ENTRANCE	doxūl دخول
EXIT	xorūg خروج
OUT OF ORDER	'attlān عطلان
CLOSED	moylaq مغلق

OPEN	maftūḥ
	مفتوح
FOR WOMEN	lel sayedāt
	للسيدات
FOR MEN	lel regāl
	للرجال

Questions

Where?	feyn? فين؟
Where to?	lefeyn? لفين؟
Where from?	men feyn? من فين؟
Why?	leyh? ليه؟
For what reason?	le'ayī sabab? لأي سبب؟
When?	emta? إمتى؟

How long?	lehadd emta? لحد إمتى؟
At what time?	fi ayī sā'a? في أي ساعة؟
How much?	bekām? بكام؟
Do you have ...?	ya tara 'andak ...? يا ترى عندك ...؟
Where is ...?	feyn ...? فين ...؟

What time is it?	el sā'a kām? الساعة كام؟
May I make a call?	momken a'mel mokalma telefoniya? ممكن أعمل مكالمة تليفونية؟
Who's there?	meyn henāk? مين هناك؟
Can I smoke here?	momken addaxen hena? ممكن أدخن هنا؟
May I ...?	momken ...? ممكن ...؟

Needs

I'd like ...	aḥebb ... أحب ...
I don't want ...	meʃ ʿāyiz ... مش عايز ...
I'm thirsty.	ana ʿaṭʃān أنا عطشان
I want to sleep.	ʿāyez anām عايز أنام
I want ...	ʿāyez ... عايز ...
to wash up	atʃaṭṭaf أتشطف
to brush my teeth	aɣsel senāny أغسل سناني
to rest a while	artāḥ ʃwaya أرتاح شوية
to change my clothes	aɣayar hodūmy أغير هدومي
to go back to the hotel	argaʿ lel fondoq أرجع للفندق
to buy ...	ʃerā' ... شراء ...
to go to ...	arūḥ le... أروح لـ...
to visit ...	azūr ... أزور ...
to meet with ...	aʿābel ... أقابل ...
to make a call	aʿmel mokalma telefoniya أعمل مكالمة تليفونية
I'm tired.	ana taʿbān أنا تعبان
We are tired.	eḥna taʿbānīn إحنا تعبانين
I'm cold.	ana bardān أنا بردان
I'm hot.	ana ḥarran أنا حران
I'm OK.	ana kowayes أنا كويس

I need to make a call.

mehtāg a'mel mokalma telefoneya
محتاج أعمل مكالمة تليفونية

I need to go to the restroom.

mehtāg arūh el hammam
محتاج أروح الحمام

I have to go.

lāzem amʃy
لازم أمشي

I have to go now.

lāzem amʃy dellwa'ty
لازم أمشي دلوقتي

Asking for directions

Excuse me, ...	ba'd ezznak, ... بعد إذنك، ...
Where is ...?	feyn ...? فين ...؟
Which way is ...?	meneyn ...? منين ...؟
Could you help me, please?	momken tesā'edny, men faḍlak? ممكن تساعدني، من فضلك؟

I'm looking for ...	ana badawwar 'la ... أنا بادور على ...
I'm looking for the exit.	baddawwar 'la ṭarīq el χorūg بادور على طريق الخروج

I'm going to ...	ana rāyeḥ le... أنا رايح لـ...
Am I going the right way to ...?	ana māʃy fel ṭarīq el ṣaḥḥ le ...? أنا ماشي في الطريق الصح لـ... ؟

Is it far?	howwa be'īd? هو بعيد؟
Can I get there on foot?	momken awṣal ḥenāk māʃy? ممكن أوصل هناك ماشي؟

Can you show me on the map?	momken tewarrīny 'lal χarīṭa? ممكن توريني على الخريطة؟
Show me where we are right now.	momken tewarrīny eḥna feyn dellwa'ty? ممكن توريني إحنا فين دلوقتي؟

Here	hena هنا
There	henāk هناك
This way	men hena من هنا

Turn right.	oddχol yemīn ادخل يمين
Turn left.	oddχol ʃemal ادخل شمال
first (second, third) turn	awwel (tāny, tālet) ʃāre' أول (تاني، تالت) شارع

to the right

'lal yemīn
على اليمين

to the left

'lal ʃemal
على الشمال

Go straight ahead.

'la ṭūl
على طول

Signs

WELCOME!	marḥaba مرحبا
ENTRANCE	doχūl دخول
EXIT	χorūg خروج

PUSH	eddfa' إدفع
PULL	ess-ḥab إسحب
OPEN	maftūḥ مفتوح
CLOSED	moχlaq مغلق

FOR WOMEN	lel sayedāt للسيدات
FOR MEN	lel regāl للرجال
GENTLEMEN, GENTS (m)	el sāda السادة
WOMEN (f)	el sayedāt السيدات

DISCOUNTS	taχfīdāt تخفيضات
SALE	okazyōn اوكازيون
FREE	maggānan مجانا
NEW!	gedīd! جديد!
ATTENTION!	ennttabeh! إنتبه!

NO VACANCIES	mafīʃ makān ما فيش مكان
RESERVED	maḥgūz محجوز
ADMINISTRATION	el edāra الإدارة
STAFF ONLY	lel 'āmelīn faqaṭ للعاملين فقط

BEWARE OF THE DOG!	ehhtaress men el kalb! !إحترس من الكلب
NO SMOKING!	mammnū' el tadҳīn! !ممنوع التدخين
DO NOT TOUCH!	mammnū' el lammss! !ممنوع اللمس
DANGEROUS	ҳaţīr خطير
DANGER	ҳaţar خطر
HIGH VOLTAGE	gohd 'āly جهد عالي
NO SWIMMING!	mammnū' el sebāḥa! !ممنوع السباحة

OUT OF ORDER	'aţţlān عطلان
FLAMMABLE	qābel lel eȷte'āl قابل للإشتعال
FORBIDDEN	mammnū' ممنوع
NO TRESPASSING!	mammnū' el taҳatty! !ممنوع التخطي
WET PAINT	ţalā' hadiis طلاء حديث

CLOSED FOR RENOVATIONS	moҳlaq lel tagdedāt مغلق للتجديدات
WORKS AHEAD	aȷҳāl fel ţarīq أشغال في الطريق
DETOUR	monḥany منحنى

Transportation. General phrases

plane	ṭayāra طيارة
train	'aṭtr قطر
bus	otobiis اوتوبيس
ferry	safina سفينة
taxi	taksi تاكسي
car	'arabiya عربية

schedule	gadwal جدول
Where can I see the schedule?	a'dar aʃūf el gadwal feyn? أقدر أشوف الجدول فين؟
workdays (weekdays)	ayām el ossbū' أيام الأسبوع
weekends	nehāyet el osbū' نهاية الأسبوع
holidays	el 'agazāt الأجازات

DEPARTURE	el saffar السفر
ARRIVAL	el woṣūl الوصول
DELAYED	mett'ẋara متأخرة
CANCELLED	molyā ملغاه

next (train, etc.)	el gayī الجاي
first	el awwel الأول
last	el 'aẋīr الأخير

When is the next ...?	emta el ... elly gayī? إللي جاي؟ ... إمتى الـ
When is the first ...?	emta awwel ...? إمتى اول ...؟

When is the last …?

emta 'āχer …?
إمتى آخر ...؟

transfer (change of trains, etc.)

tabdīl
تبديل

to make a transfer

abaddel
أبدل

Do I need to make a transfer?

hal ahtāg le tabdīl el…?
هل أحتاج لتبديل الـ...؟

Buying tickets

Where can I buy tickets?	meneyn momken aʃtery tazāker? منين ممكن أشتري تذاكر؟
ticket	tazzkara تذكرة
to buy a ticket	ʃerā' tazāker شراء تذاكر
ticket price	as'ār el tazāker أسعار التذاكر

Where to?	lefeyn? لفين؟
To what station?	le'ayī maḥaṭṭa? لأي محطة؟
I need ...	meḥtāg ... محتاج ...
one ticket	tazzkara waḥda تذكرة واحدة
two tickets	tazzkarteyn تذكرتين
three tickets	talat tazāker تلات تذاكر

one-way	zehāb faqaṭṭ ذهاب فقط
round-trip	zehāb we 'awda ذهاب وعودة
first class	daraga ūla درجة أولى
second class	daraga tanya درجة ثانية

today	el naharda النهاردة
tomorrow	bokra بكرة
the day after tomorrow	ba'd bokra بعد بكرة
in the morning	el sobḥ الصبح
in the afternoon	ba'd el zohr بعد الظهر
in the evening	bel leyl بالليل

aisle seat

korsy mammar

كرسي ممر

window seat

korsy ʃebbāk

كرسي شباك

How much?

bekām?

بكام؟

Can I pay by credit card?

momken addfaʻ be kart eʼtemān?

ممكن أدفع بكارت إئتمان؟

Bus

bus	el otobiis الأوتوبيس
intercity bus	otobiis beyn el moddon أوتوبيس بين المدن
bus stop	maḥaṭṭet el otobiis محطة الأوتوبيس
Where's the nearest bus stop?	feyn aqrab maḥaṭṭet otobiis? فين أقرب محطة أوتوبيس؟

number (bus ~, etc.)	raqam رقم
Which bus do I take to get to …?	'āxod ayī otobiis le …? أخذ أي اوتوبيس لـ...؟
Does this bus go to …?	el otobiis da beyrūḥ …? الأوتوبيس دة بيروح ...؟
How frequent are the buses?	el otobiis beyīgi kol 'add eyh? الأوتوبيس بيجي كل قد إيه؟

every 15 minutes	kol xamasstāʃar daqīqa كل 15 دقيقة
every half hour	kol noṣṣ sā'a كل نص ساعة
every hour	kol sā'a كل ساعة
several times a day	kaza marra fel yome كذا مرة في اليوم
… times a day	… marrat fell yome مرات في اليوم ...

schedule	gadwal جدول
Where can I see the schedule?	a'dar aʃūf el gadwal feyn? أقدر أشوف الجدول فين؟
When is the next bus?	emta el otobīss elly gayī? إمتى الأتوبيس إللي جاي؟
When is the first bus?	emta awwel otobiis? إمتى أول أوتوبيس؟
When is the last bus?	emta 'āxer otobiis? إمتى آخر أوتوبيس؟

stop	maḥaṭṭa محطة
next stop	el maḥaṭṭa el gaya المحطة الجاية

last stop (terminus)

axer mahatta
آخر محطة (أخر الخط)

Stop here, please.

laww samaht, wa'eff hena
لو سمحت، وقف هنا

Excuse me, this is my stop.

ba'd ezznak, di mahattetti
بعد إذنك، دي محطتي

Train

train	el 'attr القطر
suburban train	'attr el dawāhy قطر الضواحي
long-distance train	'attr el masāfāt el tawīla قطر المسافات الطويلة
train station	mahattet el 'attr محطة القطر
Excuse me, where is the exit to the platform?	ba'd ezznak, meneyn el tarīq lel rasīf بعد إذنك، منين الطريق للرصيف؟

Does this train go to ...?	el 'attr da beyrūh ...? القطر دة بيروح ...؟
next train	el 'attr el gayī? القطر الجاي؟
When is the next train?	emta el 'attr elly gayī? إمتى القطر إللي جاي؟
Where can I see the schedule?	a'dar afūf el gadwal feyn? أقدر أشوف الجدول فين؟
From which platform?	men ayī rasīf? من أي رصيف؟
When does the train arrive in ...?	emta yewsal el 'attr ...? إمتى يوصل القطر ... ؟

Please help me.	argūk sā'dny ارجوك ساعدني
I'm looking for my seat.	baddawwar 'lal korsy betā'y بادور على الكرسي بتاعي
We're looking for our seats.	ehna benndawwar 'la karāsy إحنا بندور على كراسي
My seat is taken.	el korsy betā'i mafɣūl الكرسي بتاعي مشغول
Our seats are taken.	karaseyna mafɣūla كراسينا مشغولة

I'm sorry but this is my seat.	'ann ezznak, el korsy da betā'y عن إذنك، الكرسي دة بتاعي
Is this seat taken?	el korsy da mahgūz? الكرسي دة محجوز؟
May I sit here?	momken a''od hena? ممكن أقعد هنا؟

On the train. Dialogue (No ticket)

Ticket, please.	tazāker men faḍlak
	تذاكر من فضلك
I don't have a ticket.	ma'andīʃ tazzkara
	ما عنديش تذكرة
I lost my ticket.	tazzkarty ḍā'et
	تذكرتي ضاعت
I forgot my ticket at home.	nesīt tazkarty fel beyt
	نسيت تذكرتي في البيت

You can buy a ticket from me.	momken teʃtery menny tazkara
	ممكن تشتري مني تذكرة
You will also have to pay a fine.	lāzem teddfa' ɣarāma kaman
	لازم تدفع غرامة كمان
Okay.	tamām
	تمام
Where are you going?	enta rāyeḥ feyn?
	إنت رايح فين؟
I'm going to ...	ana rāyeḥ le...
	أنا رايح لـ...

How much? I don't understand.	bekām? ana meʃ fāhem
	بكام؟ أنا مش فاهم
Write it down, please.	ektebha laww samaḥt
	إكتبها لو سمحت
Okay. Can I pay with a credit card?	tamām. momken addfa' be kredit kard?
	تمام. ممكن أدفع بكريدت كارد؟
Yes, you can.	aywā momken
	أيوة ممكن

Here's your receipt.	ettfaḍdal el īṣāl
	أتفضل الإيصال
Sorry about the fine.	'āssef bexeṣūṣ el ɣarāma
	آسف بخصوص الغرامة
That's okay. It was my fault.	mafīʃ moʃkela. di ɣaltety
	ما فيش مشكلة. دي غلطتي
Enjoy your trip.	esstammte' be reḥlatek
	استمتع برحلتك

Taxi

taxi	taksi تاكسي
taxi driver	sawwā' el taksi سواق التاكسي
to catch a taxi	'āχod taksi أخد تاكسي
taxi stand	maw'af taksi موقف تاكسي
Where can I get a taxi?	meneyn āχod taksi? منين أخد تاكسي؟

to call a taxi	an taṭṭlob taksi أن تطلب تاكسي
I need a taxi.	aḥtāg taksi أحتاج تاكسي
Right now.	al'āan الآن
What is your address (location)?	ma howa 'ennwānak? ما هو عنوانك؟
My address is ...	'ennwāny fi ... عنواني في ...
Your destination?	ettegāhak? إتجاهك؟
Excuse me, ...	ba'd ezznak, ... بعد إذنك، ...
Are you available?	enta fāḍy? إنت فاضي؟
How much is it to get to ...?	bekām arūḥ...? بكام أروح...؟
Do you know where it is?	te'raf hiya feyn? تعرف هي فين؟

Airport, please.	el maṭār men faḍlak المطار من فضلك
Stop here, please.	wa'eff hena, lavw samaḥt وقف هنا، لو سمحت
It's not here.	meʃ hena مش هنا
This is the wrong address.	da 'enwān ɣalat دة عنوان غلط
Turn left.	oddχol ʃemal ادخل شمال
Turn right.	oddχol yemīn ادخل يمين

How much do I owe you?	'layī līk ḳām? عليّ لك كام؟
I'd like a receipt, please.	'āyez īṣāl men faḍlak. عايز إيصال، من فضلك.
Keep the change.	χally el bā'y خللي الباقي

Would you please wait for me?	momken tesstannāny laww samaḥt? ممكن تستناني لو سمحت؟
five minutes	χamas daqā'eq خمس دقائق
ten minutes	'aʃar daqā'eq عشر دقائق
fifteen minutes	rob' sā'a ربع ساعة
twenty minutes	telt sā'a تلت ساعة
half an hour	noṣṣ sā'a نص ساعة

Hotel

Hello.

ahlan
أهلا

My name is ...

essmy ...
إسمي ...

I have a reservation.

'andy ḥaggz
عندي حجز

I need ...

meḥtāg ...
محتاج ...

a single room

ɣorfa moffrada
غرفة مفردة

a double room

ɣorfa mozzdawwaga
غرفة مزدوجة

How much is that?

se'raha kām?
سعرها كام؟

That's a bit expensive.

di ɣalya ʃewaya
دي غالية شوية

Do you have anything else?

'andak xayarāt tanya?
عندك خيارات تانية؟

I'll take it.

haxod-ha
ح أخدها

I'll pay in cash.

ḥaddfaʿ naqqdy
ح أدفع نقدي

I've got a problem.

ana 'andy moʃkela
أنا عندي مشكلة

My ... is broken.

... maksūr
مكسور...

My ... is out of order.

... 'aṭlān /'aṭlāna/
/عطلان /عطلانة...

TV

el televizyōn
التليفزيون

air conditioner

el takyīf
التكييف

tap

el ḥanafiya (~ 'aṭlāna)
الحنفية

---

shower

el doʃ
الدش

sink

el banyo
البانيو

safe

el xāzena (~ 'aṭlāna)
الخازنة

door lock	'effl el bāb
	قفل الباب
electrical outlet	maxrag el kahraba
	مخرج الكهربا
hairdryer	mogaffef el ʃa'r
	مجفف الشعر

I don't have ...	ma'andīʃ ...
	ما عنديش ...
water	maya
	مية
light	nūr
	نور
electricity	kahraba
	كهربا

Can you give me ...?	momken teddīny ...?
	ممكن تديني ...؟
a towel	fūta
	فوطة
a blanket	battaneya
	بطانية
slippers	ʃebʃeb
	شبشب
a robe	robe
	روب
shampoo	ʃambū
	شامبو
soap	ṣabūn
	صابون

I'd like to change rooms.	aḥebb aɣayar el oḍa
	أحب أغير الأوضة
I can't find my key.	meʃ lā'y meftāḥy
	مش لاقي مفتاحي
Could you open my room, please?	momken tefftaḥ oḍḍty men faḍlak?
	ممكن تفتح أوضتي من فضلك؟
Who's there?	meyn henāk?
	مين هناك؟
Come in!	ettfaḍḍal!
	إتفضل!
Just a minute!	daqīqa wāḥeda!
	دقيقة واحدة!
Not right now, please.	meʃ dellwa'ty men faḍlak
	مش دلوقتي من فضلك

Come to my room, please.	ta'āla oḍḍty laww samaḥt
	تعالى أوضتي لو سمحت
I'd like to order food service.	'āyez talab men xeddmet el wagabāt
	عايز طلب من خدمة الوجبات
My room number is ...	raqam oḍḍty howa ...
	رقم أوضتي هو ...

I'm leaving ...	ana mãʃy ... أنا ماشي ...
We're leaving ...	ehna maʃyīn ... إحنا ماشيين ...
right now	dellwa'ty دلوقتي
this afternoon	ba'd el zohr بعد الظهر
tonight	el leyla di الليلة دي
tomorrow	bokra بكرة
tomorrow morning	bokra el sobh بكرة الصبح
tomorrow evening	bokra bel leyl بكرة بالليل
the day after tomorrow	ba'd bokra بعد بكرة

I'd like to pay.	ahebb adfa' أحب أدفع
Everything was wonderful.	kol ʃey' kan rā'e' كل شيء كان رائع
Where can I get a taxi?	feyn momken alā'y taksi? فين ممكن ألاقي تاكسي؟
Would you call a taxi for me, please?	momken tottlob lī taksi laww samaht? ممكن تطلب لي تاكسي لو سمحت؟

Restaurant

Can I look at the menu, please?	momken aʃūf qā'ema el ṭa'ām men faḍlak? ممكن أشوف قائمة الطعام من فضلك؟
Table for one.	tarabeyza le ʃaxṣ wāḥed ترابيزة لشخص واحد
There are two (three, four) of us.	eḥna etneyn (talāta, arba'a) إحنا اتنين (ثلاثة، أربعة)

Smoking	modaxenīn مدخنين
No smoking	ɣeyr moddaxenīn غير مدخنين
Excuse me! (addressing a waiter)	laww samaḥt لو سمحت
menu	qā'emat el ṭa'ām قائمة الطعام
wine list	qā'emat el nebīz قائمة النبيذ
The menu, please.	el qā'ema, laww samaḥt القائمة، لو سمحت

Are you ready to order?	mossta'ed toṭlob? مستعد تطلب؟
What will you have?	hatāxod eh? ح تاخد إيه؟
I'll have ...	ana ḥāxod ... أنا ح أخد ...

I'm a vegetarian.	ana nabāty أنا نباتي
meat	laḥma لحم
fish	samakk سمك
vegetables	xoḍār خضار
Do you have vegetarian dishes?	'andak aṭbāq nabātiya? عندك أطباق نباتية؟
I don't eat pork.	lā 'āakol el xanzīr لا أكل الخنزير
He /she/ doesn't eat meat.	howwa /hiya/ la tākol el laḥm هو/هي/ لا تأكل اللحم

I am allergic to ...	'andy ḥasasseya men ... عندي حساسية من ...
Would you please bring me ...	momken tegīb lī ... ممكن تجيب لي...
salt | pepper | sugar	melḥ | felfel | sokkar سكر | فلفل | ملح
coffee | tea | dessert	'ahwa | ʃāy | ḥelw حلو | شاي | قهوة
water | sparkling | plain	meyāh | ɣaziya | 'adiya عادية | غازية | مياه
a spoon | fork | knife	maʻlaʻa | ʃowka | sekkīna سكينة | شوكة | ملعقة
a plate | napkin	ṭabaq | fūṭa فوطة| طبق

Enjoy your meal!	bel hana wel ʃefa بالهنا والشفا
One more, please.	waḥda kamān laww samaḥt واحدة كمان لو سمحت
It was very delicious.	kanet lazīza geddan كانت لذيذة جدا

check | change | tip	ʃīk | fakka | baʻʃīʃ بقشيش| فكة| شيك
Check, please. (Could I have the check, please?)	momken el ḥesāb laww samaḥt? ممكن الحساب لو سمحت؟
Can I pay by credit card?	momken addfaʻ ḅe kart e'temān? ممكن أدفع بكارت إئتمان؟
I'm sorry, there's a mistake here.	ana 'āssif, feyh ɣalṭa hena أنا آسف، في غلطة هنا

Shopping

Can I help you?	momken asa'dak? ممكن أساعدك؟
Do you have ...?	ya tara 'andak ...? يا ترى عندك ...؟
I'm looking for ...	ana badawwar 'la ... أنا بادور على ...
I need ...	mehtāg ... محتاج ...

I'm just looking.	ana battfarrag أنا باتفرج
We're just looking.	ehna benettfarrag إحنا بنتفرج
I'll come back later.	hāgy ba'deyn ح أجي بعدين
We'll come back later.	haneygy ba'deyn ح نيجي بعدين
discounts	sale	taxfīdāt	okazyōn أوكازيونا تخفيضات

Would you please show me ...	momken tewarrīny ... laww samaht? ممكن توريني ... لو سمحت؟
Would you please give me ...	momken teddīny ... laww samaht ممكن تديني ... لو سمحت
Can I try it on?	momken aīs? ممكن أقيس؟
Excuse me, where's the fitting room?	laww samaht, feyn el brova? لو سمحت، فين البروفا؟
Which color would you like?	'āyez ayī lone? عايز أي لون؟
size	length	maqās	tūl طول ا مقاس
How does it fit?	ya tara el maqās mazbūt? يا ترى المقاس مضبوظ؟

How much is it?	bekām? بكام؟
That's too expensive.	da ɣāly geddan دة غالي جدا
I'll take it.	haftereyh ح أشتريه
Excuse me, where do I pay?	ba'd ezznak, addfa' feyn laww samaht? بعد إذنك، أدفع فين لو سمحت؟

Will you pay in cash or credit card?	ḥateddfaʿ naqqdan walla be kart e'temān? ح تدفع نقدا ولا بكارت إئتمان؟
In cash | with credit card	naqdan | be kart e'temān بكارت إئتمان | نقدا

Do you want the receipt?	ʿāyez īṣāl? عايز إيصال؟
Yes, please.	aywā, men faḍlak أيوة، من فضلك
No, it's OK.	lā, mafīʃ moʃkela لا، ما فيش مشكلة
Thank you. Have a nice day!	ʃokran. yome saʿīd شكرا. يوم سعيد

In town

Excuse me, please.	ba'd ezznak, laww samaht بعد إذنك، لو سمحت
I'm looking for ...	ana badawwar 'la ... أنا بادور على ...

the subway	metro el anfā' مترو الأنفاق
my hotel	el fondo' betā'i الفندق بتاعي
the movie theater	el sinema السينما
a taxi stand	maw'af taksi موقف تاكسي

an ATM	makīnet ṣarraf 'āaly ماكينة صراف آلي
a foreign exchange office	maktab ṣarrafa مكتب صرافة
an internet café	maqha internet مقهى انترنت
... street	ʃāre'... ... شارع
this place	el makān da المكان دة

Do you know where ... is?	hal te'raf feyn ...? هل تعرف فين ...؟
Which street is this?	essmu eyh el ʃāre' da? اسمه إيه الشارع دة؟

Show me where we are right now.	momken tewarrīny ehna feyn dellwa'ty? ممكن توريني إحنا فين دلوقتي؟
Can I get there on foot?	momken awṣal henāk māʃy? ممكن أوصل هناك ماشي؟
Do you have a map of the city?	'andak χarīṭa lel madīna? عندك خريطة للمدينة؟

How much is a ticket to get in?	bekām tazkaret el doχūl? بكام تذكرة الدخول؟
Can I take pictures here?	momken aṣawwar hena? ممكن أصور هنا؟
Are you open?	entom fatt-hīn? إنتم فاتحين؟

When do you open?

emta betefftaḥu?
إمتى بتفتحوا؟

When do you close?

emta bete'ffelu?
إمتى بتقفلوا؟

Money

money	folūss فلوس
cash	naqdy نقدي
paper money	folūss waraqiya فلوس ورقية
loose change	fakka فكة
check | change | tip	ʃīk | fakka | baʼʃīʃ بقشيش| فكة| شيك

credit card	kart eʼtemān كارت إئتمان
wallet	mahfaza محفظة
to buy	ʃerāʼ شراء
to pay	dafʻ دفع
fine	ɣarāma غرامة
free	maggānan مجانا

Where can I buy ...?	feyn momken aʃtery ...? فين ممكن أشتري ...؟
Is the bank open now?	hal el bank fāteh dellwaʼty هل البنك فاتح دلوقتي؟
When does it open?	emta betefftah? إمتى بيفتح؟
When does it close?	emta beyeʼffel? إمتى بيقفل؟

How much?	bekām? بكام؟
How much is this?	bekām da? بكام دة؟
That's too expensive.	da ɣāly geddan دة غالي جدا

| Excuse me, where do I pay? | baʼd ezznak, addfaʼ feyn laww samaht?
بعد إذنك، أدفع فين لو سمحت؟ |
| Check, please. | el hesāb men fadlak
الحساب من فضلك |

Can I pay by credit card?	momken addfa‘ þe kart e'temān? **ممكن أدفع بكارت إئتمان؟**
Is there an ATM here?	feyh hena makīnet ṣarraf ’āaly? **فيه هنا ماكينة صراف آلي؟**
I'm looking for an ATM.	baddawwar ‘la makīnet ṣarraf ’ālly **بادور على ماكينة صراف آلي**

I'm looking for a foreign exchange office.	baddawwar ‘la maktab ṣarrāfa **بادور على مكتب صرافة**
I'd like to change ...	‘āyez aγayar ... **عايز أغير ...**
What is the exchange rate?	se‘r el ‘omla kām? **سعر العملة كام؟**
Do you need my passport?	enta meḥtāg gawāz safary? **إنت محتاج جواز سفري؟**

Time

What time is it?	el sā'a kām? الساعة كام؟
When?	emta? إمتى؟
At what time?	fi ayī sā'a? في أي ساعة؟
now | later | after ...	dellwa'ty | ba'deyn | ba'd ... ... بعد ا بعدين ا دلوقتي
one o'clock	el sā'a wahda الساعة واحدة
one fifteen	el sā'a wahda we rob' الساعة واحدة وربع
one thirty	el sā'a wahda we noṣṣ الساعة واحدة ونص
one forty-five	el sā'a etneyn ellā rob' الساعة إتنين إلا ربع
one | two | three	wahda | etneyn | talāta تلاتة اتنين وأحدة
four | five | six	arba'a | xamsa | setta ستة اخمسة أربعة
seven | eight | nine	sabb'a | tamanya | tess'a تسعة تمانية ا سبعة
ten | eleven | twelve	'aʃra | hedāʃar | etnāʃar اتناشر ا حداشر ا عشرة
in ...	fi ... في ...
five minutes	xamas daqā'eq خمس دقائق
ten minutes	'aʃar daqā'eq عشر دقائق
fifteen minutes	rob' sā'a ربع ساعة
twenty minutes	telt sā'a تلت ساعة
half an hour	noṣṣ sā'a نص ساعة
an hour	sā'a ساعة

in the morning	el sobḥ
	الصبح
early in the morning	el sobḥ badri
	الصبح بدري
this morning	el naharda el ṣobḥ
	النهاردة الصبح
tomorrow morning	bokra el sobh
	بكرة الصبح

in the middle of the day	fi noṣṣ el yome
	في نص اليوم
in the afternoon	ba'd el ẓohr
	بعد الظهر
in the evening	bel leyl
	بالليل
tonight	el leyla di
	الليلة دي

at night	bel leyl
	بالليل
yesterday	emmbāreḥ
	إمبارح
today	el naharda
	النهاردة
tomorrow	bokra
	بكرة
the day after tomorrow	ba'd bokra
	بعد بكرة

What day is it today?	el naharda eyh fel ayām?
	النهاردة إيه في الأيام؟
It's …	el naharda …
	النهاردة ...
Monday	el etneyn
	الإتنين
Tuesday	el talāt
	التلات
Wednesday	el 'arba'
	الأربع

Thursday	el χamīs
	الخميس
Friday	el gumu'ā
	الجمعة
Saturday	el sabt
	السبت
Sunday	el ḥadd
	الحد

Greetings. Introductions

Hello.

ahlan
أهلا

Pleased to meet you.

saīd be leqā'ak
سعيد بلقائك

Me too.

ana ass'ad
أنا أسعد

I'd like you to meet ...

a'arrafak be ...
أعرفك بـ ...

Nice to meet you.

forṣa saīda
فرصة سعيدة

How are you?

ezzayak?
إزيك؟

My name is ...

esmy ...
أسمي ...

His name is ...

essmu ...
إسمه ...

Her name is ...

essmaha ...
إسمها ...

What's your name?

essmak eyh?
إسمك إيه؟

What's his name?

essmu eyh?
إسمه إيه؟

What's her name?

essmaha eyh?
إسمها إيه؟

What's your last name?

essm 'ā'eltak eyh?
إسم عائلتك إيه؟

You can call me ...

te'ddar tenadīny be...
تقدر تناديني بـ...

Where are you from?

enta meneyn?
إنت منين؟

I'm from ...

ana men ...
أنا من ...

What do you do for a living?

beteʃtayal eh?
بتشتغل إيه؟

Who is this?

meyn da
مين دة

Who is he?

meyn howwa?
مين هو؟

Who is she?

meyn hiya?
مين هي؟

Who are they?

meyn homm?
مين هم؟

This is ...	da yeb'ā ... دة يبقى ...
my friend (masc.)	ṣadīqy صديقي
my friend (fem.)	ṣadīqaty صديقتي
my husband	gouzy جوزي
my wife	merāty مراتي

my father	waldy والدي
my mother	waldety والدتي
my brother	aχūya أخويا
my son	ebny إبني
my daughter	bennty بنتي

This is our son.	da ebnena دة إبننا
This is our daughter.	di benntena دي بنتنا
These are my children.	dole awwlādy دول أولادي
These are our children.	dole awwladna دول أولادنا

Farewells

Good bye!	ella alliqā' إلى اللقاء
Bye! (inform.)	salām سلام
See you tomorrow.	aʃūfak bokra أشوفك بكرة
See you soon.	aʃūfak orayeb أشوفك قريب
See you at seven.	aʃūfak el sāʻa sabʻa أشوفك الساعة سبعة
Have fun!	esstammteʻ! إستمتع!
Talk to you later.	netkallem baʻdeyn نتكلم بعدين
Have a nice weekend.	ʻoṭṭlet osbūʻ saʻīda عطلة أسبوع سعيدة
Good night.	tessbah ʻla xeyr تصبح على خير
It's time for me to go.	gā' waqt el zehāb جاء وقت الذهاب
I have to go.	lāzem amʃy لازم أمشي
I will be right back.	harga' ʻla ṭūl ح أرجع على طول
It's late.	el waqt mett'axar الوقت متأخر
I have to get up early.	lāzem aṣṣ-ha badry لازم أصحى بدري
I'm leaving tomorrow.	ana māʃy bokra أنا ماشي بكرة
We're leaving tomorrow.	ehhna maʃyīn bokra إحنا ماشيين بكرة
Have a nice trip!	rehla saʻīda! إرحلة سعيدة!
It was nice meeting you.	forṣa saʻīda فرصة سعيدة
It was nice talking to you.	saʻeddt bel kalām maʻak سعدت بالكلام معك
Thanks for everything.	ʃokran ʻla koll ʃey' شكرا على كل شيء

I had a very good time.

ana qaḍḍayt waqṭ saʿīd
أنا قضيت وقت سعيد

We had a very good time.

eḥna ʾaḍḍeyna waʾt saʿīd
إحنا قضينا وقت سعيد

It was really great.

kan bel feʿl rāʾeʿ
كان بالفعل رائع

I'm going to miss you.

hatewwhaʃīny
ح توحشني

We're going to miss you.

hatewwhaʃna
ح توحشنا

Good luck!

ḥazz saʿīd!
احظ سعيد!

Say hi to ...

taḥīāty le...
تمياتي لـ...

Foreign language

I don't understand.	ana meʃ fãhem
	أنا مش فاهم
Write it down, please.	ektebha laww samaht
	إكتبها لو سمحت
Do you speak ...?	enta betettkalem ...?
	انت بتتكلم ...؟

I speak a little bit of ...	ana battkallem ʃewaya ...
	أنا باتكلم شوية ...
English	engilīzy
	أنجليزي
Turkish	torky
	تركي
Arabic	ʿaraby
	عربي
French	faransãwy
	فرنساوي

German	almãny
	ألماني
Italian	iṭãly
	إيطالي
Spanish	asbãny
	أسباني
Portuguese	bortoɣãly
	برتغالي
Chinese	ṣīny
	صيني
Japanese	yabãny
	ياباني

Can you repeat that, please.	momken teʿīd el kalãm men faḍlak?
	ممكن تعيد الكلام من فضلك؟
I understand.	ana fãhem
	انا فاهم
I don't understand.	ana meʃ fãhem
	انا مش فاهم
Please speak more slowly.	momken tetkallem abṭaʾ laww samaht?
	ممكن تتكلم ابطأ لو سمحت؟

Is that correct? (Am I saying it right?)	keda ṣahh?
	كدة صح؟
What is this? (What does this mean?)	eh da?
	إيه دة؟

Apologies

Excuse me, please.	ba'd ezznak, laww samaḥt بعد إذنك، لو سمحت
I'm sorry.	ana 'āssif أنا آسف
I'm really sorry.	ana 'āssif beggad أنا آسف بجد
Sorry, it's my fault.	ana 'āssif, di ɣalṭeti أنا آسف، دي غلطتي
My mistake.	ɣalṭety غلطتي
May I ...?	momken ...? ممكن ...؟
Do you mind if I ...?	teddāyi' laww ...? تتضايق لو ...؟
It's OK.	mafīʃ moʃkela ما فيش مشكلة
It's all right.	kollo tamām كله تمام
Don't worry about it.	mate'la'ʃ ما تقلقش

Agreement

Yes.	aywā أيوة
Yes, sure.	aywa, akīd ايوة، أكيد
OK (Good!)	tamām تمام
Very well.	kowayīs geddan كويس جدا
Certainly!	bekol ta'kīd! إبكل تأكيد
I agree.	mewāfe' موافق

That's correct.	da ṣahīh دة صحيح
That's right.	da ṣahh دة صح
You're right.	kalāmak ṣahh كلامك صح
I don't mind.	ma'andīʃ māne' ما عنديش مانع
Absolutely right.	ṣahh tamāman صح تماماً

It's possible.	momken ممكن
That's a good idea.	di fekra kewayīsa دي فكرة كويسة
I can't say no.	ma'darʃ a'ūl la' ما أقدرش أقول لأ
I'd be happy to.	bekol sorūr حكون سعيد
With pleasure.	bekol sorūr بكل سرور

Refusal. Expressing doubt

No.	la'a
	لا
Certainly not.	akīd la'
	أكيد لأ
I don't agree.	meʃ mewāfe'
	مش موافق
I don't think so.	ma 'azzonneʃ keda
	ما أظنش كدة
It's not true.	da meʃ ṣaḥīḥ
	دة مش صحيح
You are wrong.	enta ɣalṭān
	إنت غلطان
I think you are wrong.	azonn ennak ɣalṭān
	أظن إنك غلطان
I'm not sure.	meʃ akīd
	مش أكيد
It's impossible.	da mos-taḥīl
	دة مستحيل
Nothing of the kind (sort)!	mafīʃ ḥāga keda!
	!ما فيش حاجة كدة
The exact opposite.	el 'akss tamāman
	العكس تماما
I'm against it.	ana dedd da
	أنا ضد دة
I don't care.	ma yehemmenīʃ
	ما يهمنيش
I have no idea.	ma'andīʃ fekra
	ما عنديش فكرة
I doubt it.	aʃokk fe da
	أشك في دة
Sorry, I can't.	'āssef ma 'qdarʃ
	آسف، ما أقدرش
Sorry, I don't want to.	'āssef meʃ 'ayez
	آسف، مش عايز
Thank you, but I don't need this.	ʃokran, bass ana meʃ meḥtāg loh
	شكرا، بس أنا مش محتاج له
It's getting late.	el waqt mett'aɣar
	الوقت متأخر

I have to get up early.

lāzem aṣṣ-ḥa badry

لازم أصحى بدري

I don't feel well.

ana ta'bān

أنا تعبان

Expressing gratitude

Thank you.	ʃokran شكراً
Thank you very much.	ʃokran gazīlan شكراً جزيلاً
I really appreciate it.	ana ḥa'i'i me'addar da أنا حقيقي مقدر دة
I'm really grateful to you.	ana mommtann līk geddan أنا ممتن لك جداً
We are really grateful to you.	eḥna mommtannīn līk geddan إحنا ممتنين لك جداً

Thank you for your time.	ʃokran ʿla wa'tak شكراً على وقتك
Thanks for everything.	ʃokran ʿla koll ʃey' شكراً على كل شيء
Thank you for ...	ʃokran ʿla ... شكراً على ...
your help	mosaʿdetak مساعدتك
a nice time	el waqt الوقت اللطيف

a wonderful meal	wagba rā'eʿa وجبة رائعة
a pleasant evening	amsiya mummteʿa أمسية ممتعة
a wonderful day	yome rā'eʿ يوم رائع
an amazing journey	reḥla mod-heʃa رحلة مدهشة

Don't mention it.	lā ʃokr ʿla wāgeb لا شكر على واجب
You are welcome.	el ʿafw العفو
Any time.	ayī waqt أي وقت
My pleasure.	bekol sorūr بكل سرور
Forget it.	ennsa إنسى
Don't worry about it.	mate'la'ʃ ما تقلقش

Congratulations. Best wishes

Congratulations!	ohannīk! أهنيك!
Happy birthday!	'īd milād saʿīd! عيد ميلاد سعيد!
Merry Christmas!	'īd milād saʿīd! عيد ميلاد سعيد!
Happy New Year!	sana gedīda saʿīda! سنة جديدة سعيدة!
Happy Easter!	ʃamm nessīm saʿīd! شم نسيم سعيد!
Happy Hanukkah!	hanūka saʿīda! هانوكا سعيدة!
I'd like to propose a toast.	ahebb aqtareh nefrab naxab أحب أقترح نشرب نخب
Cheers!	fi sehhettak في صحتك
Let's drink to ...!	yalla nefrab fe ...! ياللا نشرب في ...!
To our success!	nagāhna نجاحنا
To your success!	nagāhak نجاحك
Good luck!	hazz saʿīd! حظ سعيد!
Have a nice day!	nahārak saʿīd! نهارك سعيد!
Have a good holiday!	agāza tayeba! أجازة طيبة!
Have a safe journey!	trūh bel salāma! تروح بالسلامة!
I hope you get better soon!	atmanna ennak tata'āfa besor'a! أتمنى إنك تتعافى بسرعة!

Socializing

Why are you sad?	enta leyh za'lān? إنت ليه زعلان؟
Smile! Cheer up!	ebbtassem! farrfeʃ! إفرفش !إبتسم
Are you free tonight?	enta fādy el leyla di? إنت فاضي الليلة دي؟

May I offer you a drink?	momken a'zemak 'la maʃrūb? ممكن أعزمك على مشروب؟
Would you like to dance?	teḥebb torr'oṣṣ? تحب ترقص؟
Let's go to the movies.	yalla nerūḥ el sinema ياللا نروح السينما

May I invite you to …?	momken a'zemak 'la …? ممكن أعزمك على ...؟
a restaurant	maṭṭ'am مطعم
the movies	el sinema السينما
the theater	el masraḥ المسرح
go for a walk	tamʃeya تمشية

At what time?	fi ayī sā'a? في أي ساعة؟
tonight	el leyla di الليلة دي
at six	el sā'a setta الساعة ستة
at seven	el sā'a sab'a الساعة سبعة
at eight	el sā'a tamanya الساعة تمانية
at nine	el sā'a tess'a الساعة تسعة

Do you like it here?	ya tara 'agbak el makān? يا ترى عاجبك المكان؟
Are you here with someone?	enta hena ma' ḥadd? إنت هنا مع حد؟
I'm with my friend.	ana ma' ṣadīq أنا مع صديق

I'm with my friends.	ana ma' assdiqā' أنا مع أصدقاء
No, I'm alone.	lā, ana waḥḥdy لا، أنا وحدي

Do you have a boyfriend?	hal 'andak ṣadīq? هل عندك صديق؟
I have a boyfriend.	ana 'andy ṣadīq أنا عندي صديق
Do you have a girlfriend?	hal 'andak ṣadīqa? هل عندك صديقة؟
I have a girlfriend.	ana 'andy ṣadīqa أنا عندي صديقة

Can I see you again?	a'dar aʃūfak tāny? أقدر أشوفك تاني؟
Can I call you?	a'dar atteṣel bīk? أقدر أتصل بك؟
Call me. (Give me a call.)	ettaṣṣel bī إتصل بي
What's your number?	eh raqamek? إيه رقمك؟
I miss you.	wahaʃtīny وحشتني

You have a beautiful name.	essmek gamīl إسمك جميل
I love you.	oheḅbek أحبك
Will you marry me?	tettgawwezīny? تتجوزيني؟
You're kidding!	enta bett-hazzar! إنت بتهزر!
I'm just kidding.	ana bahazzar bas أنا باهزر بس

Are you serious?	enta bettettkallem gad? إنت بتتكلم جد؟
I'm serious.	ana ḡād أنا جاد
Really?!	ṣaḥīḥ? صحيح؟
It's unbelievable!	meʃ ma''ūl! مش معقول!
I don't believe you.	ana meʃ meṣṣad'āk أنا مش مصدقاك
I can't.	ma'darʃ ما أقدرش
I don't know.	ma'raʃʃ ما أعرفش
I don't understand you.	meʃ fahmāk مش فاهماك

Please go away.	men faḍlak temʃy من فضلك تمشي
Leave me alone!	sebbny lewaḥḥdy! سيبني لوحدي!

I can't stand him.	ana ḷā aṭīqo أنا لا أطيقه
You are disgusting!	enta mo'reff إنت مقرف
I'll call the police!	haṭṭlob el ʃorṭa ح أطلب الشرطة

Sharing impressions. Emotions

I like it.	ye'gebny
	يعجبني
Very nice.	laṭīf geddan
	لطيف جدا
That's great!	da rā'e'
	دة رائع
It's not bad.	da meʃ saye'
	دة مش سيء
I don't like it.	meʃ 'agebny
	مش عاجبني
It's not good.	meʃ kowayīs
	مش كويس
It's bad.	da saye'
	دة سيء
It's very bad.	da saye' geddan
	دة سيء جدا
It's disgusting.	da mo'rreff
	دة مقرف
I'm happy.	ana saʿīd
	أنا سعيد
I'm content.	ana mabsūṭ
	أنا مبسوط
I'm in love.	ana baḥebb
	أنا باحب
I'm calm.	ana hāḍy
	أنا هادي
I'm bored.	ana zaḥ'ān
	أنا زهقان
I'm tired.	ana ta'bān
	أنا تعبان
I'm sad.	ana ḥazīn
	أنا حزين
I'm frightened.	ana χāyef
	أنا خايف
I'm angry.	ana ɣadbān
	أنا غضبان
I'm worried.	ana qalqān
	أنا قلقان
I'm nervous.	ana mutawwatter
	أنا متوتر

I'm jealous. (envious)	ana γayrān
	أنا غيران
I'm surprised.	ana mutafāge'
	أنا متفاجئ
I'm perplexed.	ana morrtabek
	أنا مرتبك

Problems. Accidents

I've got a problem.	ana 'andy moʃkela أنا عندي مشكلة
We've got a problem.	ehna 'andena moʃkela إحنا عندنا مشكلة
I'm lost.	ana tāӡeh أنا تايه
I missed the last bus (train).	fātny 'āaχer otobiis فاتني آخر أوتوبيس
I don't have any money left.	meʃ fādel ma'aya flūss مش فاضل معايا فلوس

I've lost my ...	dā' menny ... betā'y ضاع مني ... بتاعي
Someone stole my ...	hadd sara' ... betā'y حد سرق ... بتاعي
passport	bassbore باسبور
wallet	mahfaza محفظة
papers	awwarā' أوراق
ticket	tazzkara تذكرة

money	folūss فلوس
handbag	ʃannta شنطة
camera	kamera كاميرا
laptop	lab tob لاب توب
tablet computer	tablet تابلت
mobile phone	telefon mahmūl تليفون محمول

Help me!	sā'dny! ساعدني!
What's happened?	eh elly hasal? إيه إللي حصل؟
fire	harīqa حريقة

shooting	ḍarrb nār ضرب نار
murder	qattl قتل
explosion	ennfegār إنفجار
fight	xenā'a خناقة

Call the police!	ettaṣel bel ʃorṭa! اتصل بالشرطة!
Please hurry up!	besor'a men faḍlak! بسرعة من فضلك!
I'm looking for the police station.	baddawwar 'la qessm el ʃorṭa بادور على قسم الشرطة
I need to make a call.	mehtāg a'mel moḳalma telefoneya محتاج أعمل مكالمة تليفونية
May I use your phone?	momken asstaxdem telefonak? ممكن أستخدم تليفونك؟

I've been …	ana kont … أنا كنت …
mugged	ettnaʃalt اتنشلت
robbed	ettsaraqt اتسرقت
raped	oɣtiṣabt اغتصبت
attacked (beaten up)	ta'arraḍt le e'tedā' تعرضت لإعتداء

Are you all right?	enta bexeyr? إنت بخير؟
Did you see who it was?	ya tara ʃoft meyn? يا ترى شفت مين؟
Would you be able to recognize the person?	te'ddar tett'arraf 'la el ʃaxṣ da? تقدر تتعرف على الشخص دة؟
Are you sure?	enta muta'kked? إنت متأكد؟

Please calm down.	argūk ehḍa أرجوك إهدا
Take it easy!	hawwen 'aleyk! اهون عليك!
Don't worry!	mate'la'ʃ! ما تقلقش!
Everything will be fine.	kol ʃey' haykūn tamām كل شيء ح يكون تمام
Everything's all right.	kol ʃey' tamām كل شيء تمام
Come here, please.	ta'āla hena laww samaḥt تعالى هنا لو سمحت

I have some questions for you.

'andy līk as'ela

عندي لك أسئلة

Wait a moment, please.

esstanna laḥza men faḍlak

إستنى لحظة من فضلك

Do you have any I.D.?

'andak raqam qawwmy

عندك رقم قومي

Thanks. You can leave now.

ʃokran. momken temʃy dellwa'ty

شكرا. ممكن تمشي دلوقتي

Hands behind your head!

eydeyk wara rāsak!

إيديك ورا راسك!

You're under arrest!

enta maqbūḍ 'aleyk!

إنت مقبوض عليك!

Health problems

Please help me.	argūk sā'dny أرجوك ساعدني
I don't feel well.	ana ta'bān أنا تعبان
My husband doesn't feel well.	gouzy ta'bān جوزي تعبان
My son ...	ebny ... إبني ...
My father ...	waldy ... والدي ...
My wife doesn't feel well.	merāty ta'bāna مراتي تعابة
My daughter ...	bennty ... بنتي ...
My mother ...	waldety ... والدتي ...
I've got a ...	ana 'andy ... أنا عندي ...
headache	ṣodā' صداع
sore throat	ehtiqān fel zore إحتقان في الزور
stomach ache	mayaṣṣ مغص
toothache	alam aṣnān ألم أسنان
I feel dizzy.	ʃā'er be dawār شاعر بدوار
He has a fever.	'andak homma عنده حمي
She has a fever.	'andaha homma عندها حمي
I can't breathe.	meʃ 'āder attnaffess مش قادر أتنفس
I'm short of breath.	meʃ 'āder attnaffess مش قادر أتنفس
I am asthmatic.	ana 'andy azzma أنا عندي أزمة
I am diabetic.	ana 'andy el sokkar أنا عندي السكر

I can't sleep.	meʃ 'āder anām
	مش قادر أنام
food poisoning	tassammom ɣezā'y
	تسمم غذائي

It hurts here.	betewwga' hena
	بتوجع هنا
Help me!	sā'edny!
	ساعدني!
I am here!	ana hena!
	أنا هنا!
We are here!	ehna hena!
	إحنا هنا!
Get me out of here!	xarragūny men hena
	خرجوني من هنا
I need a doctor.	ana mehtāg tabīb
	أنا محتاج طبيب
I can't move.	meʃ 'āder at-harrak
	مش قادر أتحرك
I can't move my legs.	meʃ 'āder aharrak reglaya
	مش قادر أحرك رجلية

I have a wound.	'andy garrhh
	عندي جرح
Is it serious?	da beggad?
	دة بجد؟
My documents are in my pocket.	awwrā'y fi geyby
	أوراقي في جيبي
Calm down!	ehhda'!
	إهدا!
May I use your phone?	momken asstaxdem telefonak?
	ممكن أستخدم تليفونك؟

Call an ambulance!	otlob 'arabeyet es'āf!
	أطلب عربية إسعاف!
It's urgent!	di hāla messta'gela!
	دي حالة مستعجلة!
It's an emergency!	di hāla tāre'a!
	دي حالة طارئة!
Please hurry up!	besor'a men fadlak!
	بسرعة من فضلك!
Would you please call a doctor?	momken tekallem doktore men fadlak?
	ممكن تكلم دكتور من فضلك؟
Where is the hospital?	feyn el mostaʃfa?
	فين المستشفى؟

How are you feeling?	hāsses be eyh dellwa'ty
	حاسس بإيه دلوقتي؟
Are you all right?	enta bexeyr?
	إنت بخير؟
What's happened?	eh elly hasal?
	إيه إللي حصل؟

I feel better now.

ana ḥāsseṣ eny aḥssan dellwa'ty

أنا حاسس إني أحسن دلوقتي

It's OK.

tamām

تمام

It's all right.

kollo tamām

كله تمام

At the pharmacy

pharmacy (drugstore)	ṣaydaliya صيدلية
24-hour pharmacy	ṣaydaliya arbʿa we ʿeʃrīn sāʿa صيدلية 24 ساعة
Where is the closest pharmacy?	feyn aqrab ṣaydaliya? فين أقرب صيدلية؟
Is it open now?	hiya fat-ḥa dellwaʾty? هي فاتحة دلوقتي؟
At what time does it open?	betefftah emta? بتفتح إمتى؟
At what time does it close?	beteʾffel emta? بتقفل إمتى؟
Is it far?	hiya beʿeyda? هي بعيدة؟
Can I get there on foot?	momken awṣal henāk māʃy? ممكن أوصل هناك ماشي؟
Can you show me on the map?	momken tewarrīny ʿlal xarīṭa? ممكن توريني على الخريطة؟
Please give me something for ...	men faḍlak eddīny hāga le... من فضلك إديني حاجة لـ...
a headache	el sodāʿ الصداع
a cough	el kohha الكحة
a cold	el bard البرد
the flu	influenza الأنفلوانزا
a fever	el ḥumma الحمى
a stomach ache	el maɣaṣṣ المغص
nausea	el ɣasayān الغثيان
diarrhea	el es-hāl الإسهال
constipation	el emsāk الإمساك
pain in the back	alam fel ẓahr ألم في الظهر

chest pain	alam fel ṣadr
	ألم في الصدر
side stitch	ɣorrza ganebiya
	غرزة جانبية
abdominal pain	alam fel baṭṭn
	ألم في البطن

pill	ḥabba
	حبة
ointment, cream	marham, krīm
	مرهم، كريم
syrup	ʃarāb
	شراب
spray	baχāχ
	بخاخ
drops	noqaṭṭ
	نقط

You need to go to the hospital.	enta meḥtāg terūḥ
	انت محتاج تروح المستشفى
health insurance	ta'mīn ṣeḥhy
	تأمين صحي
prescription	roʃetta
	روشتة
insect repellant	ṭāred lel ḥaʃarāt
	طارد للحشرات
Band Aid	blastar
	بلاستر

The bare minimum

Excuse me, ...	ba'd ezznak, ... ،بعد إذنك
Hello.	ahlan أهلا
Thank you.	ʃokran شكراً
Good bye.	ella alliqā' إلى اللقاء
Yes.	aywā أيوة
No.	la'a لأ
I don't know.	ma'raʃʃ ما أعرفش
Where?	Where to?	When?	feyn?	lefeyn?	emta? إمتى؟ I لفين؟ I فين؟

I need ...	mehtāg ... ... محتاج
I want ...	'āyez ... ... عايز
Do you have ...?	ya tara 'andak ...? يا ترى عندك... ؟
Is there a ... here?	feyh hena ...? فيه هنا ...؟
May I ...?	momken ...? ممكن ...؟
..., please (polite request)	... men fadlak ... من فضلك

I'm looking for ...	ana badawwar 'la ... ... أنا بادور على
restroom	hammām حمام
ATM	makīnet ṣarraf 'āaly ماكينة صراف آلي
pharmacy (drugstore)	ṣaydaliya صيدلية
hospital	mostaʃʃa مستشفى
police station	'essm el ʃorṭa قسم شرطة
subway	metro el anfā' مترو الأنفاق

taxi	taksi
	تاكسي
train station	mahattet el 'attr
	محطة القطر

My name is ...	essmy ...
	إسمي...
What's your name?	essmak eyh?
	اسمك إيه؟
Could you please help me?	te'ddar tesā'dny?
	تقدر تساعدني؟
I've got a problem.	ana 'andy moʃkela
	أنا عندي مشكلة
I don't feel well.	ana ta'bān
	أنا تعبان
Call an ambulance!	otlob 'arabeyet es'āf!
	أطلب عربية إسعاف!
May I make a call?	momken a'mel mokalma telefoniya?
	ممكن أعمل مكالمة تليفونية؟

I'm sorry.	ana 'āssif
	أنا آسف
You're welcome.	el 'afw
	العفو

I, me	ana
	أنا
you (inform.)	enta
	أنت
he	howwa
	هو
she	hiya
	هي
they (masc.)	homm
	هم
they (fem.)	homm
	هم
we	ehna
	احنا
you (pl)	entom
	انتم
you (sg, form.)	haddretak
	حضرتك

ENTRANCE	doxūl
	دخول
EXIT	xorūg
	خروج
OUT OF ORDER	'attlān
	عطلان
CLOSED	moylaq
	مغلق

OPEN   maftūḥ
                        مفتوح

FOR WOMEN   lel sayedāt
                        للسيدات

FOR MEN   lel regāl
                        للرجال

TOPICAL VOCABULARY

This section contains more than 3,000 of the most important words.
The dictionary will provide invaluable assistance while traveling abroad, because frequently individual words are enough for you to be understood.
The dictionary includes a convenient transcription of each foreign word

T&P Books Publishing

VOCABULARY
CONTENTS

Basic concepts	75
Numbers. Miscellaneous	81
Colours. Units of measurement	85
Main verbs	89
Time. Calendar	95
Travel. Hotel	101
Transportation	105
City	111
Clothing & Accessories	119
Everyday experience	127
Meals. Restaurant	135
Personal information. Family	145
Human body. Medicine	149
Apartment	157
The Earth. Weather	163
Fauna	175
Flora	183
Countries of the world	189

T&P Books Publishing

BASIC CONCEPTS

1. Pronouns
2. Greetings. Salutations
3. Questions
4. Prepositions
5. Function words. Adverbs. Part 1
6. Function words. Adverbs. Part 2

T&P Books Publishing

1. Pronouns

I, me	ana	أنا
you (masc.)	anta	أنت
you (fem.)	anti	أنت
he	huwa	هو
she	hiya	هي
we	naḥnu	نحن
you (to a group)	antum	أنتم
they	hum	هم

2. Greetings. Salutations

Hello! (form.)	as salāmu 'alaykum!	!السلام عليكم
Good morning!	ṣabāḥ al ҳayr!	!صباح الخير
Good afternoon!	nahārak sa'īd!	!نهارك سعيد
Good evening!	masā' al ҳayr!	!مساء الخير
to say hello	sallam	سلّم
Hi! (hello)	salām!	!سلام
greeting (n)	salām (m)	سلام
to greet (vt)	sallam 'ala	سلّم على
How are you?	kayfa ḥāluka?	كيف حالك؟
What's new?	ma aҳbārak?	ما أخبارك؟
Bye-Bye! Goodbye!	ma' as salāma!	!مع السلامة
See you soon!	ilal liqā'!	!إلى اللقاء
Farewell!	ma' as salāma!	!مع السلامة
to say goodbye	wadda'	ودّع
So long!	bay bay!	!باي باي
Thank you!	ʃukran!	!شكرًا
Thank you very much!	ʃukran ҳazīlan!	!شكرًا جزيلًا
You're welcome	'afwan	عفوا
Don't mention it!	la ʃukr 'ala wāҳib	لا شكر على واجب
It was nothing	al 'afw	العفو
Excuse me! (fam.)	'an iðnak!	!عن أذنك
Excuse me! (form.)	'afwan!	!عفوًا
to excuse (forgive)	'aðar	عذر
to apologize (vi)	i'taðar	إعتذر
My apologies	ana 'āsif	أنا آسف

I'm sorry!	la tu'āχiðni!	إلا تؤاخذني
to forgive (vt)	'afa	عفا
please (adv)	min faḍlak	من فضلك

Don't forget!	la tansa!	إلا تنس
Certainly!	ṭab'an!	إطبعًا
Of course not!	abadan!	أبدًا
Okay! (I agree)	ittafaqna!	إتّفقنا
That's enough!	kifāya!	إكفاية

3. Questions

Who?	man?	من؟
What?	māða?	ماذا؟
Where? (at, in)	ayna?	أين؟
Where (to)?	ila ayna?	إلى أين؟
From where?	min ayna?	من أين؟
When?	mata?	متى؟
Why? (What for?)	li māða?	لماذا؟
Why? (~ are you crying?)	li māða?	لماذا؟

What for?	li māða?	لماذا؟
How? (in what way)	kayfa?	كيف؟
What? (What kind of ...?)	ay?	أي؟
Which?	ay?	أي؟

To whom?	li man?	لمن؟
About whom?	'amman?	عمّن؟
About what?	'amma?	عمّا؟
With whom?	ma' man?	مع من؟

| How many? How much? | kam? | كم؟ |
| Whose? | li man? | لمن؟ |

4. Prepositions

with (accompanied by)	ma'	مع
without	bi dūn	بدون
to (indicating direction)	ila	إلى
about (talking ~ ...)	'an	عن
before (in time)	qabl	قبل
in front of ...	amām	أمام

under (beneath, below)	taḥt	تحت
above (over)	fawq	فوق
on (atop)	'ala	على
from (off, out of)	min	من
of (made from)	min	من

in (e.g., ~ ten minutes)	ba'd	بعد
over (across the top of)	'abr	عبر

5. Function words. Adverbs. Part 1

Where? (at, in)	ayna?	أين؟
here (adv)	huna	هنا
there (adv)	hunāk	هناك
somewhere (to be)	fi makānin ma	في مكان ما
nowhere (not anywhere)	la fi ay makān	لا في أي مكان
by (near, beside)	bi ʒānib	بجانب
by the window	bi ʒānib aʃ ʃubbāk	بجانب الشبّاك
Where (to)?	ila ayna?	إلى أين؟
here (e.g., come ~!)	huna	هنا
there (e.g., to go ~)	hunāk	هناك
from here (adv)	min huna	من هنا
from there (adv)	min hunāk	من هناك
close (adv)	qarīban	قريبًا
far (adv)	baʕīdan	بعيدًا
near (e.g., ~ Paris)	'ind	عند
nearby (adv)	qarīban	قريبًا
not far (adv)	ɣayr baʕīd	غير بعيد
left (adj)	al yasār	اليسار
on the left	'alaʃ ʃimāl	على الشمال
to the left	ilaʃ ʃimāl	إلى الشمال
right (adj)	al yamīn	اليمين
on the right	'alal yamīn	على اليمين
to the right	llal yamīn	إلى اليمين
in front (adv)	min al amām	من الأمام
front (as adj)	amāmiy	أمامي
ahead (the kids ran ~)	ilal amām	إلى الأمام
behind (adv)	warā'	وراء
from behind	min al warā'	من الوراء
back (towards the rear)	ilal warā'	إلى الوراء
middle	wasaṭ (m)	وسط
in the middle	fil wasaṭ	في الوسط
at the side	bi ʒānib	بجانب
everywhere (adv)	fi kull makān	في كل مكان
around (in all directions)	ḥawl	حول
from inside	min ad dāχil	من الداخل

somewhere (to go)	ila ayy makān	إلى أيّ مكان
straight (directly)	bi aqṣar ṭarīq	بأقصر طريق
back (e.g., come ~)	'īyāban	إياباً

| from anywhere | min ayy makān | من أي مكان |
| from somewhere | min makānin ma | من مكان ما |

firstly (adv)	awwalan	أوّلاً
secondly (adv)	θāniyan	ثانياً
thirdly (adv)	θāliθan	ثالثاً

suddenly (adv)	faʒ'a	فجأة
at first (in the beginning)	fil bidāya	في البداية
for the first time	li 'awwal marra	لأوّل مرّة
long before ...	qabl ... bi mudda ṭawīla	بمدّة طويلة...قبل
anew (over again)	min ʒadīd	من جديد
for good (adv)	ilal abad	إلى الأبد

never (adv)	abadan	أبداً
again (adv)	min ʒadīd	من جديد
now (adv)	al 'ān	الآن
often (adv)	kaθīran	كثيراً
then (adv)	fi ðalika al waqt	في ذلك الوقت
urgently (quickly)	'āʒilan	عاجلاً
usually (adv)	kal 'āda	كالعادة

by the way, ...	'ala fikra ...	...على فكرة
possible (that is ~)	min al mumkin	من الممكن
probably (adv)	la'alla	لعلّ
maybe (adv)	min al mumkin	من الممكن
besides ...	bil iḍāfa ila ðalik ...	...بالإضافة إلى
that's why ...	li ðalik	لذلك
in spite of ...	bir raɣm min ...	...بالرغم من
thanks to ...	bi faḍl ...	...بفضل

what (pron.)	allaði	الذي
that (conj.)	anna	أنّ
something	ʃay' (m)	شيء
anything (something)	ʃay' (m)	شيء
nothing	la ʃay'	لا شيء

who (pron.)	allaði	الذي
someone	aḥad	أحد
somebody	aḥad	أحد

nobody	la aḥad	لا أحد
nowhere (a voyage to ~)	la ila ay makān	لا إلى أي مكان
nobody's	la yaxuṣṣ aḥad	لا يخص أحداً
somebody's	li aḥad	لأحد
so (I'm ~ glad)	hakaða	هكذا
also (as well)	kaðalika	كذلك
too (as well)	ayḍan	أيضاً

6. Function words. Adverbs. Part 2

Why?	li māða?	لماذا؟
for some reason	li sababin ma	لسبب ما
because ...	li'anna ...	...لأنّ
for some purpose	li amr mā	لأمر ما

and	wa	و
or	aw	أو
but	lakin	لكن
for (e.g., ~ me)	li	لـ

too (~ many people)	kaθīran ʒiddan	كثير جدًا
only (exclusively)	faqat	فقط
exactly (adv)	biḍ ḍabṭ	بالضبط
about (more or less)	naḥw	نحو

approximately (adv)	taqrīban	تقريبًا
approximate (adj)	taqrībiy	تقريبي
almost (adv)	taqrīban	تقريبًا
the rest	al bāqi (m)	الباقي

each (adj)	kull	كلّ
any (no matter which)	ayy	أيّ
many, much (a lot of)	kaθīr	كثير
many people	kaθīr min an nās	كثير من الناس
all (everyone)	kull an nās	كل الناس

in return for ...	muqābil ...	...مقابل
in exchange (adv)	muqābil	مقابل
by hand (made)	bil yad	باليد
hardly (negative opinion)	hayhāt	هيهات

probably (adv)	la'alla	لعلّ
on purpose (intentionally)	qaṣdan	قصدا
by accident (adv)	ṣudfa	صدفة

very (adv)	ʒiddan	جدًا
for example (adv)	maθalan	مثلا
between	bayn	بين
among	bayn	بين
so much (such a lot)	haðihi al kammiyya	هذه الكمية
especially (adv)	χāṣṣa	خاصّة

NUMBERS.
MISCELLANEOUS

7. Cardinal numbers. Part 1
8. Cardinal numbers. Part 2
9. Ordinal numbers

T&P Books Publishing

7. Cardinal numbers. Part 1

0 zero	ṣifr	صفر
1 one	wāḥid	واحد
1 one (fem.)	wāḥida	واحدة
2 two	iθnān	إثنان
3 three	θalāθa	ثلاثة
4 four	arbaʿa	أريعة
5 five	xamsa	خمسة
6 six	sitta	سِتّة
7 seven	sabʿa	سبعة
8 eight	θamāniya	ثمانية
9 nine	tisʿa	تسعة
10 ten	ʿaʃara	عشرة
11 eleven	aḥad ʿaʃar	أحد عشر
12 twelve	iθnā ʿaʃar	إثنا عشر
13 thirteen	θalāθat ʿaʃar	ثلاثة عشر
14 fourteen	arbaʿat ʿaʃar	أريعة عشر
15 fifteen	xamsat ʿaʃar	خمسة عشر
16 sixteen	sittat ʿaʃar	سِتّة عشر
17 seventeen	sabʿat ʿaʃar	سبعة عشر
18 eighteen	θamāniyat ʿaʃar	ثمانية عشر
19 nineteen	tisʿat ʿaʃar	تسعة عشر
20 twenty	ʿiʃrūn	عشرون
21 twenty-one	wāḥid wa ʿiʃrūn	واحد وعشرون
22 twenty-two	iθnān wa ʿiʃrūn	إثنان وعشرون
23 twenty-three	θalāθa wa ʿiʃrūn	ثلاثة وعشرون
30 thirty	θalāθīn	ثلاثون
31 thirty-one	wāḥid wa θalāθūn	واحد وثلاثون
32 thirty-two	iθnān wa θalāθūn	إثنان وثلاثون
33 thirty-three	θalāθa wa θalāθūn	ثلاثة وثلاثون
40 forty	arbaʿūn	أربعون
41 forty-one	wāḥid wa arbaʿūn	واحد وأربعون
42 forty-two	iθnān wa arbaʿūn	إثنان وأربعون
43 forty-three	θalāθa wa arbaʿūn	ثلاثة وأربعون
50 fifty	xamsūn	خمسون
51 fifty-one	wāḥid wa xamsūn	واحد وخمسون
52 fifty-two	iθnān wa xamsūn	إثنان وخمسون
53 fifty-three	θalāθa wa xamsūn	ثلاثة وخمسون

60 sixty	sittūn	ستّون
61 sixty-one	wāḥid wa sittūn	واحد وستّون
62 sixty-two	iθnān wa sittūn	إثنان وستّون
63 sixty-three	θalāθa wa sittūn	ثلاثة وستّون

70 seventy	sab'ūn	سبعون
71 seventy-one	wāḥid wa sab'ūn	واحد وسبعون
72 seventy-two	iθnān wa sab'ūn	إثنان وسبعون
73 seventy-three	θalāθa wa sab'ūn	ثلاثة وسبعون

80 eighty	θamānūn	ثمانون
81 eighty-one	wāḥid wa θamānūn	واحد وثمانون
82 eighty-two	iθnān wa θamānūn	إثنان وثمانون
83 eighty-three	θalāθa wa θamānūn	ثلاثة وثمانون

90 ninety	tis'ūn	تسعون
91 ninety-one	wāḥid wa tis'ūn	واحد وتسعون
92 ninety-two	iθnān wa tis'ūn	إثنان وتسعون
93 ninety-three	θalāθa wa tis'ūn	ثلاثة وتسعون

8. Cardinal numbers. Part 2

100 one hundred	mi'a	مائة
200 two hundred	mi'atān	مائتان
300 three hundred	θalāθumi'a	ثلاثمائة
400 four hundred	rub'umi'a	أربعمائة
500 five hundred	xamsumi'a	خمسمائة

600 six hundred	sittumi'a	ستّمائة
700 seven hundred	sab'umi'a	سبعمائة
800 eight hundred	θamānimi'a	ثمانمائة
900 nine hundred	tis'umi'a	تسعمائة

1000 one thousand	alf	ألف
2000 two thousand	alfān	ألفان
3000 three thousand	θalāθat 'ālāf	ثلاثة آلاف
10000 ten thousand	'aʃarat 'ālāf	عشرة آلاف
one hundred thousand	mi'at alf	مائة ألف
million	milyūn (m)	مليون
billion	milyār (m)	مليار

9. Ordinal numbers

first (adj)	awwal	أوّل
second (adj)	θāni	ثان
third (adj)	θāliθ	ثالث
fourth (adj)	rābi'	رابع
fifth (adj)	xāmis	خامس

sixth (adj)	sādis	سادس
seventh (adj)	sābiʿ	سابع
eighth (adj)	θāmin	ثامن
ninth (adj)	tāsiʿ	تاسع
tenth (adj)	ʿāʃir	عاشر

COLOURS. UNITS OF MEASUREMENT

10. Colors
11. Units of measurement
12. Containers

T&P Books Publishing

10. Colors

color	lawn (m)	لون
shade (tint)	daraʒat al lawn (m)	درجة اللون
hue	ṣabɣit lūn (f)	لون
rainbow	qaws quzaḥ (m)	قوس قزح
white (adj)	abyaḍ	أبيض
black (adj)	aswad	أسود
gray (adj)	ramādiy	رمادي
green (adj)	axḍar	أخضر
yellow (adj)	aṣfar	أصفر
red (adj)	aḥmar	أحمر
blue (adj)	azraq	أزرق
light blue (adj)	azraq fātiḥ	أزرق فاتح
pink (adj)	wardiy	وردي
orange (adj)	burtuqāliy	برتقالي
violet (adj)	banafsaʒiy	بنفسجي
brown (adj)	bunniy	بني
golden (adj)	ðahabiy	ذهبي
silvery (adj)	fiḍḍiy	فضي
beige (adj)	bɛːʒ	بيج
cream (adj)	ʿāʒiy	عاجي
turquoise (adj)	fayrūziy	فيروزي
cherry red (adj)	karaziy	كرزي
lilac (adj)	laylakiy	ليلكي
crimson (adj)	qirmiziy	قرمزي
light (adj)	fātiḥ	فاتح
dark (adj)	ɣāmiq	غامق
bright, vivid (adj)	zāhi	زاه
colored (pencils)	mulawwan	ملون
color (e.g., ~ film)	mulawwan	ملون
black-and-white (adj)	abyaḍ wa aswad	أبيض وأسود
plain (one-colored)	waḥīd al lawn, sāda	وحيد اللون، سادة
multicolored (adj)	mutaʿaddid al alwān	متعدد الألوان

11. Units of measurement

weight	wazn (m)	وزن
length	ṭūl (m)	طول

width	'arḍ (m)	عرض
height	irtifā' (m)	إرتفاع
depth	'umq (m)	عمق
volume	ḥaʒm (m)	حجم
area	misāḥa (f)	مساحة

gram	grām (m)	جرام
milligram	milliɣrām (m)	مليغرام
kilogram	kiluɣrām (m)	كيلوغرام
ton	ṭunn (m)	طنّ
pound	raṭl (m)	رطل
ounce	ūnṣa (f)	أونصة

meter	mitr (m)	متر
millimeter	millimitr (m)	مليمتر
centimeter	santimitr (m)	سنتيمتر
kilometer	kilumitr (m)	كيلومتر
mile	mīl (m)	ميل

inch	būṣa (f)	بوصة
foot	qadam (f)	قدم
yard	yārda (f)	ياردة

square meter	mitr murabba' (m)	متر مربّع
hectare	hiktār (m)	هكتار
liter	litr (m)	لتر
degree	daraʒa (f)	درجة
volt	vūlt (m)	فولت
ampere	ambīr (m)	أمبير
horsepower	ḥiṣān (m)	حصان

quantity	kammiyya (f)	كمّية
a little bit of ...	qalīl ...	قليل...
half	niṣf (m)	نصف
dozen	iθnā 'aʃar (f)	إثنا عشر
piece (item)	waḥda (f)	وحدة

| size | ḥaʒm (m) | حجم |
| scale (map ~) | miqyās (m) | مقياس |

minimal (adj)	al adna	الأدنى
the smallest (adj)	al aṣɣar	الأصغر
medium (adj)	mutawassiṭ	متوسّط
maximal (adj)	al aqsa	الأقصى
the largest (adj)	al akbar	الأكبر

12. Containers

| canning jar (glass ~) | barṭamān (m) | برطمان |
| can | tanaka (f) | تنكة |

bucket	ʒardal (m)	جردل
barrel	barmīl (m)	برميل
wash basin (e.g., plastic ~)	ḥawḍ lil ɣasīl (m)	حوض للغسيل
tank (100L water ~)	xazzān (m)	خزّان
hip flask	zamzamiyya (f)	زمزميّة
jerrycan	ʒirikan (m)	جركن
tank (e.g., tank car)	xazzān (m)	خزّان
mug	mãgg (m)	ماجّ
cup (of coffee, etc.)	finʒãn (m)	فنجان
saucer	ṭabaq finʒãn (m)	طبق فنجان
glass (tumbler)	kubbāya (f)	كبّاية
wine glass	ka's (f)	كأس
stock pot (soup pot)	kassirũlla (f)	كاسرولة
bottle (~ of wine)	zuʒãʒa (f)	زجاجة
neck (of the bottle, etc.)	ʿunq (m)	عنق
carafe (decanter)	dawraq zuʒãʒiy (m)	دورق زجاجيّ
pitcher	ibrīq (m)	إبريق
vessel (container)	inã' (m)	إناء
pot (crock, stoneware ~)	aṣīṣ (m)	أصيص
vase	vãza (f)	فازة
bottle (perfume ~)	zuʒãʒa (f)	زجاجة
vial, small bottle	zuʒãʒa (f)	زجاجة
tube (of toothpaste)	umbūba (f)	أنبوبة
sack (bag)	kīs (m)	كيس
bag (paper ~, plastic ~)	kīs (m)	كيس
pack (of cigarettes, etc.)	ʿulba (f)	علبة
box (e.g., shoebox)	ʿulba (f)	علبة
crate	ṣundū' (m)	صندوق
basket	salla (f)	سلّة

MAIN VERBS

13. The most important verbs. Part 1
14. The most important verbs. Part 2
15. The most important verbs. Part 3
16. The most important verbs. Part 4

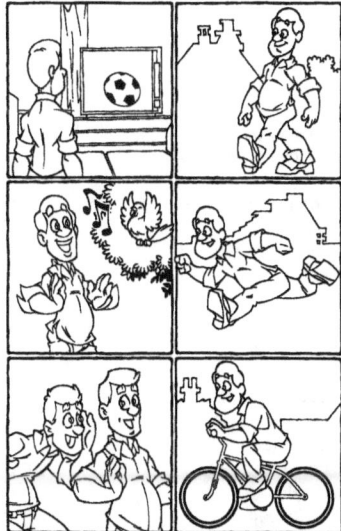

T&P Books Publishing

to advise (vt)	naṣaḥ	نصح
to agree (say yes)	ittafaq	إتّفق
to answer (vi, vt)	aʒāb	أجاب
to apologize (vi)	iʿtaðar	إعتذر
to arrive (vi)	waṣal	وصل
to ask (~ oneself)	saʾal	سأل
to ask (~ sb to do sth)	ṭalab	طلب
to be (vi)	kān	كان
to be afraid	χāf	خاف
to be hungry	arād an yaʾkul	أراد أن يأكل
to be interested in ...	ihtamm	إهتمّ
to be needed	kān maṭlūb	كان مطلوبا
to be surprised	indahaʃ	إندهش
to be thirsty	arād an yaʃrab	أراد أن يشرب
to begin (vt)	badaʾ	بدأ
to belong to ...	χaṣṣ	خصّ
to boast (vi)	tabāha	تباهى
to break (split into pieces)	kasar	كسر
to call (~ for help)	istaɣāθ	إستغاث
can (v aux)	istaṭāʿ	إستطاع
to catch (vt)	amsak	أمسك
to change (vt)	ɣayyar	غيّر
to choose (select)	iχtār	إختار
to come down (the stairs)	nazil	نزل
to compare (vt)	qāran	قارن
to complain (vi, vt)	ʃaka	شكا
to confuse (mix up)	iχtalaṭ	إختلط
to continue (vt)	istamarr	إستمرّ
to control (vt)	taḥakkam	تحكّم
to cook (dinner)	ḥaḍḍar	حضّر
to cost (vt)	kallaf	كلّف
to count (add up)	ʿadd	عدّ
to count on ...	iʿtamad ʿala ...	إعتمد على...
to create (vt)	χalaq	خلق
to cry (weep)	baka	بكى

14. The most important verbs. Part 2

to deceive (vi, vt)	χada'	خدع
to decorate (tree, street)	zayyan	زيّن
to defend (a country, etc.)	dāfa'	دافع
to demand (request firmly)	ṭālib	طالب
to dig (vt)	ḥafar	حفر
to discuss (vt)	nāqaʃ	ناقش
to do (vt)	'amal	عمل
to doubt (have doubts)	ʃakk fi	شكّ في
to drop (let fall)	awqa'	أوقع
to enter (room, house, etc.)	daχal	دخل
to exist (vi)	kān mawʒūd	كان موجودًا
to expect (foresee)	tanabba'	تنبّأ
to explain (vt)	ʃaraḥ	شرح
to fall (vi)	saqaṭ	سقط
to find (vt)	waʒad	وجد
to finish (vt)	atamm	أتمّ
to fly (vi)	ṭār	طار
to follow ... (come after)	taba'	تبع
to forget (vi, vt)	nasiy	نسي
to forgive (vt)	'afa	عفا
to give (vt)	a'ṭa	أعطى
to give a hint	a'ṭa talmīḥ	أعطى تلميحًا
to go (on foot)	maʃa	مشى
to go for a swim	sabaḥ	سبح
to go out (for dinner, etc.)	χaraʒ	خرج
to guess (the answer)	χamman	خمّن
to have (vt)	malak	ملك
to have breakfast	afṭar	أفطر
to have dinner	ta'aʃʃa	تعشّى
to have lunch	tayadda	تغدّى
to hear (vt)	sami'	سمع
to help (vt)	sā'ad	ساعد
to hide (vt)	χaba'	خبّأ
to hope (vi, vt)	tamanna	تمنّى
to hunt (vi, vt)	iṣṭād	إصطاد
to hurry (vi)	ista'ʒal	إستعجل

15. The most important verbs. Part 3

to inform (vt)	aχbar	أخبر
to insist (vi, vt)	aṣarr	أصرّ

to insult (vt)	ahān	أهان
to invite (vt)	da'a	دعا
to joke (vi)	mazaḥ	مزح

to keep (vt)	ḥafaẓ	حفظ
to keep silent	sakat	سكت
to kill (vt)	qatal	قتل
to know (sb)	'araf	عرف
to know (sth)	'araf	عرف
to laugh (vi)	ḍaḥik	ضحك

to liberate (city, etc.)	ḥarrar	حرّر
to like (I like ...)	a'ʒab	أعجب
to look for ... (search)	baḥaθ	بحث
to love (sb)	aḥabb	أحبّ
to make a mistake	aҳṭa'	أخطأ

to manage, to run	adār	أدار
to mean (signify)	'ana	عنى
to mention (talk about)	ðakar	ذكر
to miss (school, etc.)	ɣāb	غاب
to notice (see)	lāḥaẓ	لاحظ

to object (vi, vt)	i'taraḍ	إعترض
to observe (see)	rāqab	راقب
to open (vt)	fataḥ	فتح
to order (meal, etc.)	ṭalab	طلب
to order (mil.)	amar	أمر
to own (possess)	malak	ملك

to participate (vi)	iʃtarak	إشترك
to pay (vi, vt)	dafa'	دفع
to permit (vt)	raҳҳaṣ	رخّص
to plan (vt)	ҳaṭṭaṭ	خطّط
to play (children)	la'ib	لعب

to pray (vi, vt)	ṣalla	صلّى
to prefer (vt)	faḍḍal	فضّل
to promise (vt)	wa'ad	وعد
to pronounce (vt)	naṭaq	نطق
to propose (vt)	iqtaraḥ	إقترح
to punish (vt)	'āqab	عاقب

16. The most important verbs. Part 4

to read (vi, vt)	qara'	قرأ
to recommend (vt)	naṣaḥ	نصح
to refuse (vi, vt)	rafaḍ	رفض
to regret (be sorry)	nadim	ندم
to rent (sth from sb)	ista'ʒar	إستأجر

to repeat (say again)	karrar	كرّر
to reserve, to book	ḥaʒaz	حجز
to run (vi)	ʒara	جرى
to save (rescue)	anqað	أنقذ
to say (~ thank you)	qāl	قال
to scold (vt)	wabbaχ	وبّخ
to see (vt)	ra'a	رأى
to sell (vt)	bā'	باع
to send (vt)	arsal	أرسل
to shoot (vi)	aṭlaq an nār	أطلق النار
to shout (vi)	ṣaraχ	صرخ
to show (vt)	'araḍ	عرض
to sign (document)	waqqa'	وقّع
to sit down (vi)	ʒalas	جلس
to smile (vi)	ibtasam	إبتسم
to speak (vi, vt)	takallam	تكلّم
to steal (money, etc.)	saraq	سرق
to stop (for pause, etc.)	waqaf	وقف
to stop (please ~ calling me)	tawaqqaf	توقّف
to study (vt)	daras	درس
to swim (vi)	sabaḥ	سبح
to take (vt)	aχað	أخذ
to think (vi, vt)	ẓann	ظنّ
to threaten (vt)	haddad	هدّد
to touch (with hands)	lamas	لمس
to translate (vt)	tarʒam	ترجم
to trust (vt)	waθiq	وثق
to try (attempt)	ḥāwal	حاول
to turn (e.g., ~ left)	in'aṭaf	إنعطف
to underestimate (vt)	istaχaff	إستخفّ
to understand (vt)	fahim	فهم
to unite (vt)	waḥḥad	وحّد
to wait (vt)	intaẓar	إنتظر
to want (wish, desire)	arād	أراد
to warn (vt)	ḥaððar	حذّر
to work (vi)	'amal	عمل
to write (vt)	katab	كتب
to write down	katab	كتب

T&P BOOKS

TIME. CALENDAR

17. Weekdays
18. Hours. Day and night
19. Months. Seasons

T&P Books Publishing

17. Weekdays

Monday	yawm al iθnayn (m)	يوم الإثنين
Tuesday	yawm aθ θulāθā' (m)	يوم الثلاثاء
Wednesday	yawm al arbi'ā' (m)	يوم الأربعاء
Thursday	yawm al χamīs (m)	يوم الخميس
Friday	yawm al ʒum'a (m)	يوم الجمعة
Saturday	yawm as sabt (m)	يوم السبت
Sunday	yawm al aḥad (m)	يوم الأحد
today (adv)	al yawm	اليوم
tomorrow (adv)	γadan	غداً
the day after tomorrow	ba'd γad	بعد غد
yesterday (adv)	ams	أمس
the day before yesterday	awwal ams	أوّل أمس
day	yawm (m)	يوم
working day	yawm 'amal (m)	يوم عمل
public holiday	yawm al 'uṭla ar rasmiyya (m)	يوم العطلة الرسمية
day off	yawm 'uṭla (m)	يوم عطلة
weekend	ayyām al 'uṭla (pl)	أيام العطلة
all day long	ṭūl al yawm	طول اليوم
the next day (adv)	fil yawm at tāli	في اليوم التالي
two days ago	min yawmayn	قبل يومين
the day before	fil yawm as sābiq	في اليوم السابق
daily (adj)	yawmiy	يومي
every day (adv)	yawmiyyan	يومياً
week	usbū' (m)	أسبوع
last week (adv)	fil isbū' al māḍi	في الأسبوع الماضي
next week (adv)	fil isbū' al qādim	في الأسبوع القادم
weekly (adj)	usbū'iy	أسبوعي
every week (adv)	usbū'iyyan	أسبوعياً
twice a week	marratayn fil usbū'	مرّتين في الأسبوع
every Tuesday	kull yawm aθ θulaθā'	كل يوم الثلاثاء

18. Hours. Day and night

morning	ṣabāḥ (m)	صباح
in the morning	fiṣ ṣabāḥ	في الصباح
noon, midday	ẓuhr (m)	ظهر
in the afternoon	ba'd aẓ ẓuhr	بعد الظهر

evening	masā' (m)	مساء
in the evening	fil masā'	في المساء
night	layl (m)	ليل
at night	bil layl	بالليل
midnight	muntaṣif al layl (m)	منتصف الليل

second	θāniya (f)	ثانية
minute	daqīqa (f)	دقيقة
hour	sā'a (f)	ساعة
half an hour	niṣf sā'a (m)	نصف ساعة
a quarter-hour	rub' sā'a (f)	ربع ساعة
fifteen minutes	χamsat 'aʃar daqīqa	خمس عشرة دقيقة
24 hours	yawm kāmil (m)	يوم كامل

sunrise	ʃurūq aʃ ʃams (m)	شروق الشمس
dawn	faʒr (m)	فجر
early morning	ṣabāḥ bākir (m)	صباح باكر
sunset	ɣurūb aʃ ʃams (m)	غروب الشمس

early in the morning	fis ṣabāḥ al bākir	في الصباح الباكر
this morning	al yawm fiṣ ṣabāḥ	اليوم في الصباح
tomorrow morning	ɣadan fiṣ ṣabāḥ	غدًا في الصباح

this afternoon	al yawm ba'd aẓ ẓuhr	اليوم بعد الظهر
in the afternoon	ba'd aẓ ẓuhr	بعد الظهر
tomorrow afternoon	ɣadan ba'd aẓ ẓuhr	غدًا بعد الظهر

| tonight (this evening) | al yawm fil masā' | اليوم في المساء |
| tomorrow night | ɣadan fil masā' | غدًا في المساء |

at 3 o'clock sharp	fis sā'a aθ θāliθa tamāman	في الساعة الثالثة تماما
about 4 o'clock	fis sā'a ar rābi'a taqrīban	في الساعة الرابعة تقريبا
by 12 o'clock	ḥattas sā'a aθ θāniya 'aʃara	حتى الساعة الثانية عشرة

in 20 minutes	ba'd 'iʃrīn daqīqa	بعد عشرين دقيقة
in an hour	ba'd sā'a	بعد ساعة
on time (adv)	fi maw'idih	في موعده

a quarter of ...	illa rub'	إلا ربع
within an hour	ṭiwāl sā'a	طوال الساعة
every 15 minutes	kull rub' sā'a	كل ربع ساعة
round the clock	layl nahār	ليل نهار

19. Months. Seasons

January	yanāyir (m)	يناير
February	fibrāyir (m)	فبراير
March	māris (m)	مارس
April	abrīl (m)	أبريل
May	māyu (m)	مايو

June	yūnyu (m)	يونيو
July	yūlyu (m)	يوليو
August	aɣusṭus (m)	أغسطس
September	sibtambar (m)	سبتمبر
October	uktūbir (m)	أكتوبر
November	nuvimbar (m)	نوفمبر
December	disimbar (m)	ديسمبر

spring	rabī' (m)	ربيع
in spring	fir rabī'	في الربيع
spring (as adj)	rabī'iy	ربيعي

summer	ṣayf (m)	صيف
in summer	fiṣ ṣayf	في الصيف
summer (as adj)	ṣayfiy	صيفي

fall	xarīf (m)	خريف
in fall	fil xarīf	في الخريف
fall (as adj)	xarīfiy	خريفيّ

winter	ʃitāʾ (m)	شتاء
in winter	fiʃ ʃitāʾ	في الشتاء
winter (as adj)	ʃitawiy	شتويّ

month	ʃahr (m)	شهر
this month	fi haða aʃ ʃahr	في هذا الشهر
next month	fiʃ ʃahr al qādim	في الشهر القادم
last month	fiʃ ʃahr al māḍi	في الشهر الماضي

a month ago	qabl ʃahr	قبل شهر
in a month (a month later)	ba'd ʃahr	بعد شهر
in 2 months (2 months later)	ba'd ʃahrayn	بعد شهرين
the whole month	ṭūl aʃ ʃahr	طول الشهر
all month long	ʃahr kāmil	شهر كامل

monthly (~ magazine)	ʃahriy	شهريّ
monthly (adv)	kull ʃahr	كل شهر
every month	kull ʃahr	كل شهر
twice a month	marratayn fiʃ ʃahr	مرّتين في الشهر

year	sana (f)	سنة
this year	fi haðihi as sana	في هذه السنة
next year	fis sana al qādima	في السنة القادمة
last year	fis sana al māḍiya	في السنة الماضية

a year ago	qabla sana	قبل سنة
in a year	ba'd sana	بعد سنة
in two years	ba'd sanatayn	بعد سنتين
the whole year	ṭūl as sana	طول السنة
all year long	sana kāmila	سنة كاملة
every year	kull sana	كل سنة

annual (adj)	sanawiy	سنويّ
annually (adv)	kull sana	كل سنة
4 times a year	arba' marrāt fis sana	أربع مرّات في السنة
date (e.g., today's ~)	tarīχ (m)	تاريخ
date (e.g., ~ of birth)	tarīχ (m)	تاريخ
calendar	taqwīm (m)	تقويم
half a year	niṣf sana (m)	نصف سنة
six months	niṣf sana (m)	نصف سنة
season (summer, etc.)	faṣl (m)	فصل
century	qarn (m)	قرن

TRAVEL. HOTEL

20. Trip. Travel
21. Hotel
22. Sightseeing

T&P Books Publishing

20. Trip. Travel

tourism, travel	siyāḥa (f)	سياحة
tourist	sā'iḥ (m)	سائح
trip, voyage	riḥla (f)	رحلة
adventure	muɣāmara (f)	مغامرة
trip, journey	riḥla (f)	رحلة
vacation	ʿutla (f)	عطلة
to be on vacation	ʿindahu ʿutla	عنده عطلة
rest	istirāḥa (f)	إستراحة
train	qiṭār (m)	قطار
by train	bil qiṭār	بالقطار
airplane	ṭā'ira (f)	طائرة
by airplane	biṭ ṭā'ira	بالطائرة
by car	bis sayyāra	بالسيّارة
by ship	bis safīna	بالسفينة
luggage	aʃ ʃunaṭ (pl)	الشنط
suitcase	ḥaqībat safar (f)	حقيبة سفر
luggage cart	ʿarabat ʃunaṭ (f)	عربة شنط
passport	ʒawāz as safar (m)	جواز السفر
visa	ta'ʃīra (f)	تأشيرة
ticket	taðkira (f)	تذكرة
air ticket	taðkirat ṭā'ira (f)	تذكرة طائرة
guidebook	dalīl (m)	دليل
map (tourist ~)	χarīṭa (f)	خريطة
area (rural ~)	mintaqa (f)	منطقة
place, site	makān (m)	مكان
exotica (n)	ɣarāba (f)	غرابة
exotic (adj)	ɣarīb	غريب
amazing (adj)	mudhiʃ	مدهش
group	maʒmūʿa (f)	مجموعة
excursion, sightseeing tour	ʒawla (f)	جولة
guide (person)	murʃid (m)	مرشد

21. Hotel

hotel	funduq (m)	فندق
motel	mutīl (m)	موتيل

three-star (~ hotel)	θalāθat nuʒūm	ثلاثة نجوم
five-star	χamsat nuʒūm	خمسة نجوم
to stay (in a hotel, etc.)	nazal	نزل

room	ɣurfa (f)	غرفة
single room	ɣurfa li ʃaχṣ wāḥid (f)	غرفة لشخص واحد
double room	ɣurfa li ʃaχṣayn (f)	غرفة لشخصين
to book a room	ḥaʒaz ɣurfa	حجز غرفة

| half board | waʒbitān fil yawm (du) | وجبتان في اليوم |
| full board | θalāθ waʒabāt fil yawm | ثلاث وجبات في اليوم |

with bath	bi ḥawḍ al istiḥmām	بحوض الإستحمام
with shower	bid duʃ	بالدوش
satellite television	tilivizyūn faḍā'iy (m)	تلفزيون فضائيّ
air-conditioner	takyīf (m)	تكييف
towel	fūṭa (f)	فوطة
key	miftāḥ (m)	مفتاح

administrator	mudīr (m)	مدير
chambermaid	'āmilat tanẓīf ɣuraf (f)	عاملة تنظيف غرف
porter, bellboy	ḥammāl (m)	حمّال
doorman	bawwāb (m)	بوّاب

restaurant	maṭ'am (m)	مطعم
pub, bar	bār (m)	بار
breakfast	fuṭūr (m)	فطور
dinner	'aʃā' (m)	عشاء
buffet	bufīh (m)	بوفيه

| lobby | radha (f) | ردهة |
| elevator | miṣ'ad (m) | مصعد |

| DO NOT DISTURB | ar raʒā' 'adam al iz'āʒ | الرجاء عدم الإزعاج |
| NO SMOKING | mamnū' at tadχīn | ممنوع التدخين |

22. Sightseeing

monument	timθāl (m)	تمثال
fortress	qal'a (f), ḥiṣn (m)	قلعة, حصن
palace	qaṣr (m)	قصر
castle	qal'a (f)	قلعة
tower	burʒ (m)	برج
mausoleum	ḍarīḥ (m)	ضريح

architecture	handasa mi'māriyya (f)	هندسة معماريّة
medieval (adj)	min al qurūn al wusṭa	من القرون الوسطى
ancient (adj)	qadīm	قديم
national (adj)	waṭaniy	وطنيّ
famous (monument, etc.)	maʃhūr	مشهور

tourist	sā'iḥ (m)	سائح
guide (person)	murʃid (m)	مرشد
excursion, sightseeing tour	ʒawla (f)	جولة
to show (vt)	ʿaraḍ	عرض
to tell (vt)	ḥaddaθ	حدّث
to find (vt)	waʒad	وجد
to get lost (lose one's way)	ḍāʿ	ضاع
map (e.g., subway ~)	χarīṭa (f)	خريطة
map (e.g., city ~)	χarīṭa (f)	خريطة
souvenir, gift	tiðkār (m)	تذكار
gift shop	maḥall hadāya (m)	محلّ هدايا
to take pictures	ṣawwar	صوّر
to have one's picture taken	taṣawwar	تصوّر

BOOKS

T&P

TRANSPORTATION

23. Airport
24. Airplane
25. Train
26. Ship

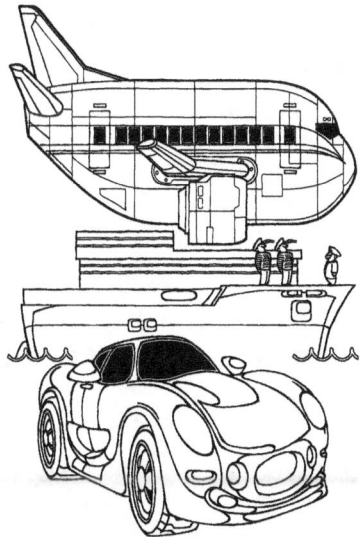

T&P Books Publishing

23. Airport

airport	maṭār (m)	مطار
airplane	ṭā'ira (f)	طائرة
airline	ʃarikat ṭayarān (f)	شركة طيران
air traffic controller	marāqib al ḥaraka al ӡawwiyya (pl)	مراقب الحركة الجويّة
departure	muɣādara (f)	مغادرة
arrival	wuṣūl (m)	وصول
to arrive (by plane)	waṣal	وصل
departure time	waqt al muɣādara (m)	وقت المغادرة
arrival time	waqt al wuṣūl (m)	وقت الوصول
to be delayed	ta'aҳҳar	تأخّر
flight delay	ta'aҳҳur ar riḥla (m)	تأخّر الرحلة
information board	lawḥat al maʿlūmāt (f)	لوحة المعلومات
information	istiʿlāmāt (pl)	إستعلامات
to announce (vt)	aʿlan	أعلن
flight (e.g., next ~)	riḥla (f)	رحلة
customs	ӡamārik (pl)	جمارك
customs officer	muwaẓẓaf al ӡamārik (m)	موظف الجمارك
customs declaration	taṣrīḥ ӡumrukiy (m)	تصريح جمركيّ
to fill out (vt)	mala'	ملأ
to fill out the declaration	mala' at taṣrīḥ	ملأ التصريح
passport control	taftīʃ al ӡawāzāt (m)	تفتيش الجوازات
luggage	aʃ ʃunaṭ (pl)	الشنط
hand luggage	ʃunaṭ al yad (pl)	شنط اليد
luggage cart	ʿarabat ʃunaṭ (f)	عربة شنط
landing	hubūṭ (m)	هبوط
landing strip	mamarr al hubūṭ (m)	ممرّ الهبوط
to land (vi)	habaṭ	هبط
airstairs	sullam aṭ ṭā'ira (m)	سلّم الطائرة
check-in	tasӡīl (m)	تسجيل
check-in counter	makān at tasӡīl (m)	مكان التسجيل
to check-in (vi)	saӡӡal	سجّل
boarding pass	biṭāqat ṣuʿūd (f)	بطاقة صعود
departure gate	bawwābat al muɣādara (f)	بوّابة المغادرة
transit	tranzīt (m)	ترانزيت

to wait (vt)	intazar	إنتظر
departure lounge	qā'at al muɣādara (f)	قاعة المغادرة
to see off	wadda'	ودّع
to say goodbye	wadda'	ودّع

24. Airplane

airplane	tā'ira (f)	طائرة
air ticket	taðkirat tā'ira (f)	تذكرة طائرة
airline	ʃarikat tayarān (f)	شركة طيران
airport	matār (m)	مطار
supersonic (adj)	xāriq liș șawt	خارق للصوت

captain	qā'id aț țā'ira (m)	قائد الطائرة
crew	tāqim (m)	طاقم
pilot	tayyār (m)	طيّار
flight attendant (fem.)	muḍīfat tayarān (f)	مضيفة طيران
navigator	mallāḥ (m)	ملّاح

wings	aʒniḥa (pl)	أجنحة
tail	ðayl (m)	ذيل
cockpit	kabīna (f)	كابينة
engine	mutūr (m)	موتور
undercarriage (landing gear)	'aʒalāt al hubūț (pl)	عجلات الهبوط
turbine	turbīna (f)	تربينة

propeller	mirwaḥa (f)	مروحة
black box	musaʒʒil aț țayarān (m)	مسجّل الطيران
yoke (control column)	'aʒalat qiyāda (f)	عجلة قيادة
fuel	wuqūd (m)	وقود

safety card	bițāqat as salāma (f)	بطاقة السلامة
oxygen mask	qinā' uksiʒīn (m)	قناع أوكسجين
uniform	libās muwaḥḥad (m)	لباس موحّد
life vest	sutrat naʒāt (f)	سترة نجاة
parachute	miʒallat hubūț (f)	مظلّة هبوط

takeoff	iqlā' (m)	إقلاع
to take off (vi)	aqla'at	أقلعت
runway	madraʒ aț țā'irāt (m)	مدرج الطائرات

visibility	ru'ya (f)	رؤية
flight (act of flying)	tayarān (m)	طيران
altitude	irtifā' (m)	إرتفاع
air pocket	ʒayb hawā'iy (m)	جيب هوائيّ

seat	maq'ad (m)	مقعد
headphones	sammā'āt ra'siya (pl)	سمّاعات رأسيّة
folding tray (tray table)	șīniyya qābila liț țayy (f)	صينية قابلة للطيّ

| airplane window | ʃubbāk aṭ ṭā'ira (m) | شبّاك الطائرة |
| aisle | mamarr (m) | ممرّ |

25. Train

train	qiṭār (m)	قطار
commuter train	qiṭār (m)	قطار
express train	qiṭār sarīʿ (m)	قطار سريع
diesel locomotive	qāṭirat dīzil (f)	قاطرة ديزل
steam locomotive	qāṭira buxāriyya (f)	قاطرة بخاريّة

| passenger car | ʿaraba (f) | عربة |
| dining car | ʿarabat al maṭʿam (f) | عربة المطعم |

rails	quḍubān (pl)	قضبان
railroad	sikka ḥadīdiyya (f)	سكّة حديديّة
railway tie	ʿāriḍa (f)	عارضة

platform (railway ~)	raṣīf (m)	رصيف
track (~ 1, 2, etc.)	xaṭṭ (m)	خطّ
semaphore	simafūr (m)	سيمافور
station	maḥaṭṭa (f)	محطّة

engineer (train driver)	sā'iq (m)	سائق
porter (of luggage)	ḥammāl (m)	حمّال
car attendant	mas'ūl ʿarabat al qiṭār (m)	مسؤول عربة القطار
passenger	rākib (m)	راكب
conductor (ticket inspector)	kamsariy (m)	كمسريّ

| corridor (in train) | mamarr (m) | ممرّ |
| emergency brake | farāmil aṭ ṭawāri' (pl) | فرامل الطوارئ |

compartment	yurfa (f)	غرفة
berth	sarīr (m)	سرير
upper berth	sarīr ʿulwiy (m)	سرير علويّ
lower berth	sarīr sufliy (m)	سرير سفليّ
bed linen, bedding	aytiyat as sarīr (pl)	أغطية السرير

ticket	taðkira (f)	تذكرة
schedule	ʒadwal (m)	جدول
information display	lawḥat maʿlūmāt (f)	لوحة معلومات

to leave, to depart	yādar	غادر
departure (of train)	muyādara (f)	مغادرة
to arrive (ab. train)	waṣal	وصل
arrival	wuṣūl (m)	وصول

| to arrive by train | waṣal bil qiṭār | وصل بالقطار |
| to get on the train | rakib al qiṭār | ركب القطار |

to get off the train	nazil min al qiṭār	نزل من القطار
train wreck	ḥiṭām qiṭār (m)	حطام قطار
to derail (vi)	χaraʒ ʿan χaṭṭ sayrih	خرج عن خطَ سيره
steam locomotive	qāṭira buχāriyya (f)	قاطرة بخاريَة
stoker, fireman	ʿataʃʒiy (m)	عطشجي
firebox	furn al muḥarrik (m)	فرن المحرَك
coal	faḥm (m)	فحم

26. Ship

ship	safīna (f)	سفينة
vessel	safīna (f)	سفينة
steamship	bāχira (f)	باخرة
riverboat	bāχira nahriyya (f)	باخرة نهريَة
cruise ship	bāχira siyaḥiyya (f)	باخرة سياحيَة
cruiser	ṭarrād (m)	طرَاد
yacht	yaχt (m)	يخت
tugboat	qāṭira (f)	قاطرة
barge	ṣandal (m)	صندل
ferry	ʿabbāra (f)	عبَارة
sailing ship	safīna ʃirāʿiyya (m)	سفينة شراعيَة
brigantine	markab ʃirāʿiy (m)	مركب شراعيَ
ice breaker	muḥaṭṭimat ʒalīd (f)	محطَمة جليد
submarine	ɣawwāṣa (f)	غوَاصة
boat (flat-bottomed ~)	markab (m)	مركب
dinghy	zawraq (m)	زورق
lifeboat	qārib naʒāt (m)	قارب نجاة
motorboat	lanʃ (m)	لنش
captain	qubṭān (m)	قبطان
seaman	baḥḥār (m)	بحَار
sailor	baḥḥār (m)	بحَار
crew	ṭāqim (m)	طاقم
boatswain	raʾīs al baḥḥāra (m)	رئيس البحَارة
ship's boy	ṣabiy as safīna (m)	صبي السفينة
cook	ṭabbāχ (m)	طبَاخ
ship's doctor	ṭabīb as safīna (m)	طبيب السفينة
deck	saṭḥ as safīna (m)	سطح السفينة
mast	sāriya (f)	سارية
sail	ʃirāʿ (m)	شراع
hold	ʿambar (m)	عنبر
bow (prow)	muqaddama (m)	مقدَمة

stern	mu'axirat as safina (f)	مؤخّرة السفينة
oar	miʒðāf (m)	مجذاف
screw propeller	mirwaḥa (f)	مروحة

cabin	kabīna (f)	كابينة
wardroom	ɣurfat al istirāḥa (f)	غرفة الإستراحة
engine room	qism al 'ālāt (m)	قسم الآلات
bridge	burʒ al qiyāda (m)	برج القيادة
radio room	ɣurfat al lāsilkiy (f)	غرفة اللاسلكيّ
wave (radio)	mawʒa (f)	موجة
logbook	siʒil as safina (m)	سجل السفينة

spyglass	minʒār (m)	منظار
bell	ʒaras (m)	جرس
flag	'alam (m)	علم

| hawser (mooring ~) | ḥabl (m) | حبل |
| knot (bowline, etc.) | 'uqda (f) | عقدة |

| deckrails | drabizīn (m) | درابزين |
| gangway | sullam (m) | سلّم |

anchor	mirsāt (f)	مرساة
to weigh anchor	rafa' mirsāt	رفع مرساة
to drop anchor	rasa	رسا
anchor chain	silsilat mirsāt (f)	سلسلة مرساة

port (harbor)	mīnā' (m)	ميناء
quay, wharf	marsa (m)	مرسى
to berth (moor)	rasa	رسا
to cast off	aqla'	أقلع

trip, voyage	riḥla (f)	رحلة
cruise (sea trip)	riḥla baḥriyya (f)	رحلة بحرية
course (route)	masār (m)	مسار
route (itinerary)	ṭarīq (m)	طريق

fairway (safe water channel)	maʒra milāḥiy (m)	مجرى ملاحيّ
shallows	miyāh ḍaḥla (f)	مياه ضحلة
to run aground	ʒanaḥ	جنح

storm	'āṣifa (f)	عاصفة
signal	iʃāra (f)	إشارة
to sink (vi)	ɣariq	غرق
Man overboard!	saqaṭ raʒul min as safīna!	!سقط رجل من السفينة
SOS (distress signal)	nidā' iɣāθa (m)	نداء إغاثة
ring buoy	ṭawq naʒāt (m)	طوق نجاة

T&P BOOKS

CITY

27. Urban transportation
28. City. Life in the city
29. Urban institutions
30. Signs
31. Shopping

T&P Books Publishing

27. Urban transportation

bus	bāṣ (m)	باص
streetcar	trām (m)	ترام
trolley bus	truli bāṣ (m)	ترولي باص
route (of bus, etc.)	χaṭṭ (m)	خطّ
number (e.g., bus ~)	raqm (m)	رقم
to go by ...	rakib ...	...ركب
to get on (~ the bus)	rakib	ركب
to get off ...	nazil min	نزل من
stop (e.g., bus ~)	mawqif (m)	موقف
next stop	al maḥaṭṭa al qādima (f)	المحطّة القادمة
terminus	āχir maḥaṭṭa (f)	آخر محطّة
schedule	ʒadwal (m)	جدول
to wait (vt)	inṭazar	إنتظر
ticket	taðkira (f)	تذكرة
fare	uʒra (f)	أجرة
cashier (ticket seller)	ṣarrāf (m)	صرّاف
ticket inspection	taftīʃ taðkira (m)	تفتيش تذكرة
ticket inspector	mufattiʃ taðākir (m)	مفتّش تذاكر
to be late (for ...)	ta'aχχar	تأخّر
to miss (~ the train, etc.)	ta'aχχar	تأخّر
to be in a hurry	ista'ʒal	إستعجل
taxi, cab	taksi (m)	تاكسي
taxi driver	sā'iq taksi (m)	سائق تاكسي
by taxi	bit taksi	بالتاكسي
taxi stand	mawqif taksi (m)	موقف تاكسي
to call a taxi	kallam tāksi	كلّم تاكسي
to take a taxi	aχað taksi	أخذ تاكسي
traffic	ḥarakat al murūr (f)	حركة المرور
traffic jam	zaḥmat al murūr (f)	زحمة المرور
rush hour	sā'at að ðurwa (f)	ساعة الذروة
to park (vi)	awqaf	أوقف
to park (vt)	awqaf	أوقف
parking lot	mawqif as sayyārāt (m)	موقف السيارات
subway	mitru (m)	مترو
station	maḥaṭṭa (f)	محطّة
to take the subway	rakib al mitru	ركب المترو

train	qiṭār (m)	قطار
train station	maḥaṭṭat qiṭār (f)	محطة قطار

28. City. Life in the city

city, town	madīna (f)	مدينة
capital city	'āṣima (f)	عاصمة
village	qarya (f)	قرية
city map	xarīṭat al madīna (f)	خريطة المدينة
downtown	markaz al madīna (m)	مركز المدينة
suburb	ḍāḥiya (f)	ضاحية
suburban (adj)	aḍ ḍawāḥi	الضواحي
outskirts	aṭrāf al madīna (pl)	أطراف المدينة
environs (suburbs)	ḍawāḥi al madīna (pl)	ضواحي المدينة
city block	ḥayy (m)	حي
residential block (area)	ḥayy sakaniy (m)	حي سكني
traffic	ḥarakat al murūr (f)	حركة المرور
traffic lights	iʃārāt al murūr (pl)	إشارات المرور
public transportation	wasāʼil an naql (pl)	وسائل النقل
intersection	taqāṭuʻ (m)	تقاطع
crosswalk	maʻbar al muʃāt (m)	معبر المشاة
pedestrian underpass	nafaq muʃāt (m)	نفق مشاة
to cross (~ the street)	'abar	عبر
pedestrian	māʃi (m)	ماش
sidewalk	raṣīf (m)	رصيف
bridge	ʒisr (m)	جسر
embankment (river walk)	kurnīʃ (m)	كورنيش
fountain	nāfūra (f)	نافورة
allée (garden walkway)	mamʃa (m)	ممشى
park	ḥadīqa (f)	حديقة
boulevard	bulvār (m)	بولفار
square	maydān (m)	ميدان
avenue (wide street)	ʃāriʻ (m)	شارع
street	ʃāriʻ (m)	شارع
side street	zuqāq (m)	زقاق
dead end	ṭarīq masdūd (m)	طريق مسدود
house	bayt (m)	بيت
building	mabna (m)	مبنى
skyscraper	nāṭiḥat saḥāb (f)	ناطحة سحاب
facade	wāʒiha (f)	واجهة
roof	saqf (m)	سقف
window	ʃubbāk (m)	شباك

arch	qaws (m)	قوس
column	'amūd (m)	عمود
corner	zāwiya (f)	زاوية

store window	vatrīna (f)	فترينة
signboard (store sign, etc.)	lāfita (f)	لافتة
poster	mulṣaq (m)	ملصق
advertising poster	mulṣaq i'lāniy (m)	ملصق إعلاني
billboard	lawḥat i'lānāt (f)	لوحة إعلانات

garbage, trash	zubāla (f)	زبالة
trashcan (public ~)	ṣundūq zubāla (m)	صندوق زبالة
to litter (vi)	rama zubāla	رمى زبالة
garbage dump	mazbala (f)	مزبلة

phone booth	kuʃk tilifūn (m)	كشك تليفون
lamppost	'amūd al miṣbāḥ (m)	عمود المصباح
bench (park ~)	dikka (f), kursiy (m)	دكّة, كرسيّ

police officer	ʃurṭiy (m)	شرطيّ
police	ʃurṭa (f)	شرطة
beggar	ʃaḥḥāð (m)	شحّاذ
homeless (n)	mutaʃarrid (m)	متشرّد

29. Urban institutions

store	maḥall (m)	محلّ
drugstore, pharmacy	ṣaydaliyya (f)	صيدليّة
eyeglass store	al adawāt al baṣariyya (pl)	الأدوات البصريّة
shopping mall	markaz tiʒāriy (m)	مركز تجاريّ
supermarket	subirmarkit (m)	سوبرماركت

bakery	maxbaz (m)	مخبز
baker	xabbāz (m)	خبّاز
pastry shop	dukkān ḥalawāniy (m)	دكّان حلوانيّ
grocery store	baqqāla (f)	بقّالة
butcher shop	malḥama (f)	ملحمة

produce store	dukkān xuḍār (m)	دكّان خضار
market	sūq (f)	سوق

coffee house	kafé (m), maqha (m)	كافيه, مقهى
restaurant	maṭ'am (m)	مطعم
pub, bar	ḥāna (f)	حانة
pizzeria	maṭ'am pizza (m)	مطعم بيتزا

hair salon	ṣālūn ḥilāqa (m)	صالون حلاقة
post office	maktab al barīd (m)	مكتب البريد
dry cleaners	tanẓīf ʒāff (m)	تنظيف جافّ
photo studio	istūdiyu taṣwīr (m)	إستوديو تصوير

shoe store	maḥall aḥðiya (m)	محلّ أحذية
bookstore	maḥall kutub (m)	محلّ كتب
sporting goods store	maḥall riyāḍiy (m)	محلّ رياضيّ
clothes repair shop	maḥall χiyāṭat malābis (m)	محلّ خياطة ملابس
formal wear rental	maḥall ta'ʒīr malābis rasmiyya (m)	محلّ تأجير ملابس رسمية
video rental store	maḥal ta'ʒīr vidiyu (m)	محلّ تأجير فيديو
circus	sirk (m)	سيرك
zoo	ḥadīqat al ḥayawān (f)	حديقة حيوان
movie theater	sinima (f)	سينما
museum	matḥaf (m)	متحف
library	maktaba (f)	مكتبة
theater	masraḥ (m)	مسرح
opera (opera house)	ubra (f)	أوبرا
nightclub	malha layliy (m)	ملهى ليليّ
casino	kazinu (m)	كازينو
mosque	masʒid (m)	مسجد
synagogue	kanīs ma'bad yahūdiy (m)	كنيس معبد يهوديّ
cathedral	katidrā'iyya (f)	كاتدرائيّة
temple	ma'bad (m)	معبد
church	kanīsa (f)	كنيسة
college	kulliyya (m)	كلّيّة
university	ʒāmi'a (f)	جامعة
school	madrasa (f)	مدرسة
prefecture	muqāṭa'a (f)	مقاطعة
city hall	baladiyya (f)	بلديّة
hotel	funduq (m)	فندق
bank	bank (m)	بنك
embassy	safāra (f)	سفارة
travel agency	ʃarikat siyāḥa (f)	شركة سياحة
information office	maktab al isti'lāmāt (m)	مكتب الإستعلامات
currency exchange	ṣarrāfa (f)	صرّافة
subway	mitru (m)	مترو
hospital	mustaʃfa (m)	مستشفى
gas station	maḥaṭṭat banzīn (f)	محطّة بنزين
parking lot	mawqif as sayyārāt (m)	موقف السيّارات

30. Signs

| signboard (store sign, etc.) | lāfita (f) | لافتة |
| notice (door sign, etc.) | bayān (m) | بيان |

poster	mulṣaq i'lāniy (m)	ملصق إعلانيّ
direction sign	'alāmat ittiʒāh (f)	علامة إتّجاه
arrow (sign)	'alāmat iʃāra (f)	علامة إشارة
caution	taḥðīr (m)	تحذير
warning sign	lāfitat taḥðīr (f)	لافتة تحذير
to warn (vt)	ḥaððar	حذّر
rest day (weekly ~)	yawm 'uṭla (m)	يوم عطلة
timetable (schedule)	ʒadwal (m)	جدول
opening hours	awqāt al 'amal (pl)	أوقات العمل
WELCOME!	ahlan wa sahlan!	أهلًا وسهلًا
ENTRANCE	duχūl	دخول
EXIT	χurūʒ	خروج
PUSH	idfa'	إدفع
PULL	isḥab	إسحب
OPEN	maftūḥ	مفتوح
CLOSED	muχlaq	مغلق
WOMEN	lis sayyidāt	للسيدات
MEN	lir riʒāl	للرجال
DISCOUNTS	χaṣm	خصم
SALE	taχfiḍāt	تخفيضات
NEW!	ʒadīd!	جديد!
FREE	maʒʒānan	مجّانًا
ATTENTION!	intibāh!	إنتباه!
NO VACANCIES	kull al amākin maḥʒūza	كل الأماكن محجوزة
RESERVED	maḥʒūz	محجوز
ADMINISTRATION	idāra	إدارة
STAFF ONLY	lil 'āmilīn faqaṭ	للعاملين فقط
BEWARE OF THE DOG!	iḥðar wuʒūd al kalb	إحذر وجود الكلب
NO SMOKING	mamnū' at tadχīn	ممنوع التدخين
DO NOT TOUCH!	'adam al lams	عدم اللمس
DANGEROUS	χaṭīr	خطير
DANGER	χaṭar	خطر
HIGH VOLTAGE	tayyār 'āli	تيّار عالي
NO SWIMMING!	as sibāḥa mamnū'a	السياحة ممنوعة
OUT OF ORDER	mu'aṭṭal	معطّل
FLAMMABLE	sarī' al iʃti'āl	سريع الإشتعال
FORBIDDEN	mamnū'	ممنوع
NO TRESPASSING!	mamnū' al murūr	ممنوع المرور
WET PAINT	iḥðar ṭilā' ɣayr ʒāff	إحذر طلاء غير جاف

31. Shopping

to buy (purchase)	iʃtara	إشترى
purchase	ʃay' (m)	شيء
to go shopping	iʃtara	إشترى
shopping	ʃubinɣ (m)	شوبينغ
to be open (ab. store)	maftūḥ	مفتوح
to be closed	muɣlaq	مغلق
footwear, shoes	aḥðiya (pl)	أحذية
clothes, clothing	malābis (pl)	ملابس
cosmetics	mawādd at taʒmīl (pl)	مواد التجميل
food products	ma'kūlāt (pl)	مأكولات
gift, present	hadiyya (f)	هديّة
salesman	bā'i' (m)	بائع
saleswoman	bā'i'a (f)	بائعة
check out, cash desk	ṣundū' ad daf' (m)	صندوق الدفع
mirror	mir'āt (f)	مرآة
counter (store ~)	minḍada (f)	منضدة
fitting room	ɣurfat al qiyās (f)	غرفة القياس
to try on	ʒarrab	جرّب
to fit (ab. dress, etc.)	nāsab	ناسب
to like (I like ...)	a'ʒab	أعجب
price	si'r (m)	سعر
price tag	tikit as si'r (m)	تيكت السعر
to cost (vt)	kallaf	كلّف
How much?	bikam?	بكم؟
discount	χaṣm (m)	خصم
inexpensive (adj)	ɣayr ɣāli	غير غال
cheap (adj)	raχīṣ	رخيص
expensive (adj)	ɣāli	غال
It's expensive	haða ɣāli	هذا غال
rental (n)	isti'ʒār (m)	إستئجار
to rent (~ a tuxedo)	ista'ʒar	إستأجر
credit (trade credit)	i'timān (m)	إئتمان
on credit (adv)	bid dayn	بالدين

CLOTHING & ACCESSORIES

32. Outerwear. Coats
33. Men's & women's clothing
34. Clothing. Underwear
35. Headwear
36. Footwear
37. Personal accessories
38. Clothing. Miscellaneous
39. Personal care. Cosmetics
40. Watches. Clocks

T&P Books Publishing

32. Outerwear. Coats

clothes	malābis (pl)	ملابس
outerwear	malābis fawqāniyya (pl)	ملابس فوقانيّة
winter clothing	malābis ʃitawiyya (pl)	ملابس شتويّة
coat (overcoat)	miʿṭaf (m)	معطف
fur coat	miʿṭaf farw (m)	معطف فرو
fur jacket	ʒakīt farw (m)	جاكيت فرو
down coat	ḥaʃiyyat rīʃ (m)	حشية ريش
jacket (e.g., leather ~)	ʒākīt (m)	جاكيت
raincoat (trenchcoat, etc.)	miʿṭaf lil maṭar (m)	معطف للمطر
waterproof (adj)	ṣāmid lil māʾ	صامد للماء

33. Men's & women's clothing

shirt (button shirt)	qamīṣ (m)	قميص
pants	banṭalūn (m)	بنطلون
jeans	ʒīnz (m)	جينز
suit jacket	sutra (f)	سترة
suit	badla (f)	بدلة
dress (frock)	fustān (m)	فستان
skirt	tannūra (f)	تنّورة
blouse	blūza (f)	بلوزة
knitted jacket (cardigan, etc.)	kardigān (m)	كارديجان
jacket (of woman's suit)	ʒākīt (m)	جاكيت
T-shirt	ti ʃirt (m)	تي شيرت
shorts (short trousers)	ʃūrt (m)	شورت
tracksuit	badlat at tadrīb (f)	بدلة التدريب
bathrobe	θawb ḥammām (m)	ثوب حمّام
pajamas	biʒāma (f)	بيجاما
sweater	bulūvir (m)	بلوفر
pullover	bulūvir (m)	بلوفر
vest	ṣudayriy (m)	صديريّ
tailcoat	badlat sahra (f)	بدلة سهرة
tuxedo	smūkin (m)	سموكن
uniform	zayy muwaḥḥad (m)	زي موحّد
workwear	θiyāb al ʿamal (m)	ثياب العمل

| overalls | uvirūl (m) | اوفرول |
| coat (e.g., doctor's smock) | θawb (m) | ثوب |

34. Clothing. Underwear

underwear	malābis dāχiliyya (pl)	ملابس داخليّة
boxers, briefs	sirwāl dāχiliy riǧāliy (m)	سروال داخلي رجاليّ
panties	sirwāl dāχiliy nisā'iy (m)	سروال داخلي نسائيّ
undershirt (A-shirt)	qamīṣ bila aqmām (m)	قميص بلا أكمام
socks	ǧawārib (pl)	جوارب

nightgown	qamīṣ nawm (m)	قميص نوم
bra	hammālat ṣadr (f)	حمّالة صدر
knee highs	ǧawārib ṭawīla (pl)	جوارب طويلة
(knee-high socks)		

pantyhose	ǧawārib kulūn (pl)	جوارب كولون
stockings (thigh highs)	ǧawārib nisā'iyya (pl)	جوارب نسائية
bathing suit	libās sibāḥa (m)	لباس سباحة

35. Headwear

hat	qubba'a (f)	قبّعة
fedora	burnayṭa (f)	برنيطة
baseball cap	kāb baysbūl (m)	كاب بيسبول
flatcap	qubba'a musaṭṭaḥa (f)	قبّعة مسطحة

beret	birīh (m)	بيريه
hood	γiṭā' (m)	غطاء
panama hat	qubba'at banāma (f)	قبّعة بناما
knit cap (knitted hat)	qubbā'a maḥbūka (m)	قبّعة محبوكة

| headscarf | 'īǧārb (m) | إيشارب |
| women's hat | burnayṭa (f) | برنيطة |

hard hat	χūða (f)	خوذة
garrison cap	kāb (m)	كاب
helmet	χūða (f)	خوذة

| derby | qubba'at dirbi (f) | قبّعة ديربي |
| top hat | qubba'a 'āliya (f) | قبّعة عالية |

36. Footwear

footwear	aḥðiya (pl)	أحذية
shoes (men's shoes)	ǧazma (f)	جزمة
shoes (women's shoes)	ǧazma (f)	جزمة

| boots (e.g., cowboy ~) | būt (m) | بوت |
| slippers | ʃibʃib (m) | شبشب |

tennis shoes (e.g., Nike ~)	ḥiðā' riyāḍiy (m)	حذاء رياضيّ
sneakers	kutʃi (m)	كوتشي
(e.g., Converse ~)		
sandals	ṣandal (pl)	صندل

cobbler (shoe repairer)	iskāfiy (m)	إسكافيّ
heel	ka'b (m)	كعب
pair (of shoes)	zawʒ (m)	زوج

| shoestring | ʃarīṭ (m) | شريط |
| to lace (vt) | rabaṭ | ربط |

| shoehorn | labbāsat ḥiðā' (f) | لبّاسة حذاء |
| shoe polish | warnīʃ al ḥiðā' (m) | ورنيش الحذاء |

37. Personal accessories

gloves	quffāz (m)	قفّاز
mittens	quffāz muɣlaq (m)	قفّاز مغلق
scarf (muffler)	'īʃārb (m)	إيشارب

glasses (eyeglasses)	nazzāra (f)	نظّارة
frame (eyeglass ~)	iṭār (m)	إطار
umbrella	ʃamsiyya (f)	شمسيّة
walking stick	'aṣa (f)	عصا

| hairbrush | furʃat ʃa'r (f) | فرشة شعر |
| fan | mirwaḥa yadawiyya (f) | مروحة يدويّة |

| tie (necktie) | karavatta (f) | كرافتة |
| bow tie | babyūn (m) | بيبون |

| suspenders | ḥammāla (f) | حمّالة |
| handkerchief | mandīl (m) | منديل |

| comb | miʃṭ (m) | مشط |
| barrette | dabbūs (m) | دبّوس |

| hairpin | bansa (m) | بنسة |
| buckle | bukla (f) | بكلة |

| belt | ḥizām (m) | حزام |
| shoulder strap | ḥammalat al katf (f) | حمّالة الكتف |

bag (handbag)	ʃanṭa (f)	شنطة
purse	ʃanṭat yad (f)	شنطة يد
backpack	ḥaqībat ẓahr (f)	حقيبة ظهر

38. Clothing. Miscellaneous

fashion	mūḍa (f)	موضة
in vogue (adj)	fil mūḍa	في الموضة
fashion designer	musammim azyā' (m)	مصمّم أزياء

collar	yāqa (f)	ياقة
pocket	ʒayb (m)	جيب
pocket (as adj)	ʒayb	جيب
sleeve	kumm (m)	كمّ
hanging loop	ʻallāqa (f)	علّاقة
fly (on trousers)	lisān (m)	لسان

zipper (fastener)	zimām munzaliq (m)	زمام منزلق
fastener	miʃbak (m)	مشبك
button	zirr (m)	زرّ
buttonhole	ʻurwa (f)	عروة
to come off (ab. button)	waqaʻ	وقع

to sew (vi, vt)	xāṭ	خاط
to embroider (vi, vt)	ṭarraz	طرّز
embroidery	taṭrīz (m)	تطريز
sewing needle	ibra (f)	إبرة
thread	xayṭ (m)	خيط
seam	darz (m)	درز

to get dirty (vi)	tawassax	توسّخ
stain (mark, spot)	buqʻa (f)	بقعة
to crease, crumple (vi)	takarmaʃ	تكرمش
to tear, to rip (vt)	qaṭṭaʻ	قطّع
clothes moth	ʻuθθa (f)	عثّة

39. Personal care. Cosmetics

toothpaste	maʻʒūn asnān (m)	معجون أسنان
toothbrush	furʃat asnān (f)	فرشة أسنان
to brush one's teeth	naẓẓaf al asnān	نظّف الأسنان

razor	mūs ḥilāqa (m)	موس حلاقة
shaving cream	krīm ḥilāqa (m)	كريم حلاقة
to shave (vi)	ḥalaq	حلق

| soap | ṣābūn (m) | صابون |
| shampoo | ʃāmbū (m) | شامبو |

scissors	maqaṣṣ (m)	مقصّ
nail file	mibrad (m)	ميرد
nail clippers	milqaṭ (m)	ملقط
tweezers	milqaṭ (m)	ملقط

cosmetics	mawādd at taʒmīl (pl)	مواد التجميل
face mask	mask (m)	ماسك
manicure	manikūr (m)	مانيكور
to have a manicure	ʿamal manikūr	عمل مانيكور
pedicure	badikīr (m)	باديكير
make-up bag	ḥaqībat adawāt at taʒmīl (f)	حقيبة أدوات التجميل
face powder	budrat waʒh (f)	بودرة وجه
powder compact	ʿulbat būdra (f)	علبة بودرة
blusher	aḥmar χudūd (m)	أحمر خدود
perfume (bottled)	ʿiṭr (m)	عطر
toilet water (lotion)	kulūnya (f)	كولونيا
lotion	lusiyun (m)	لوسيون
cologne	kulūniya (f)	كولونيا
eyeshadow	ay ʃaduw (m)	اي شادو
eyeliner	kuḥl al ʿuyūn (m)	كحل العيون
mascara	maskara (f)	ماسكارا
lipstick	aḥmar ʃifāh (m)	أحمر شفاه
nail polish, enamel	mulammiʿ al azāfir (m)	ملمّع الاظافر
hair spray	muθabbit aʃ ʃaʿr (m)	مثبّت الشعر
deodorant	muzīl rawā'iḥ (m)	مزيل روائح
cream	krīm (m)	كريم
face cream	krīm lil waʒh (m)	كريم للوجه
hand cream	krīm lil yadayn (m)	كريم لليدين
anti-wrinkle cream	krīm muḍādd lit taʒāʿīd (m)	كريم مضاد للتجاعيد
day cream	krīm an nahār (m)	كريم النهار
night cream	krīm al layl (m)	كريم الليل
day (as adj)	nahāriy	نهاري
night (as adj)	layliy	ليلي
tampon	tambūn (m)	تانبون
toilet paper (toilet roll)	waraq ḥammām (m)	ورق حمّام
hair dryer	muʒaffif ʃaʿr (m)	مجفف شعر

40. Watches. Clocks

watch (wristwatch)	sāʿa (f)	ساعة
dial	waʒh as sāʿa (m)	وجه الساعة
hand (of clock, watch)	ʿaqrab as sāʿa (m)	عقرب الساعة
metal watch band	siwār sāʿa maʿdaniyya (m)	سوار ساعة معدنية
watch strap	siwār sāʿa (m)	سوار ساعة
battery	baṭṭāriyya (f)	بطّارية
to be dead (battery)	tafarraχ	تفرّغ
to change a battery	χayyar al baṭṭāriyya	غيّر البطّارية
to run fast	sabaq	سبق

to run slow	ta'axxar	تَأَخَّر
wall clock	sā'at ḥā'iṭ (f)	ساعة حائط
hourglass	sā'a ramliyya (f)	ساعة رملِيّة
sundial	sā'a ʃamsiyya (f)	ساعة شمسِيّة
alarm clock	munabbih (m)	منبّه
watchmaker	sa'ātiy (m)	ساعاتيّ
to repair (vt)	aṣlaḥ	أصلح

EVERYDAY EXPERIENCE

41. Money
42. Post. Postal service
43. Banking
44. Telephone. Phone conversation
45. Cell phone
46. Stationery
47. Foreign languages

T&P Books Publishing

money	nuqūd (pl)	نقود
currency exchange	taḥwīl ʿumla (m)	تحويل عملة
exchange rate	siʿr aṣ ṣarf (m)	سعر الصرف
ATM	ṣarrāf ʾāliy (m)	صرّاف آليّ
coin	qiṭʿa naqdiyya (f)	قطعة نقدية
dollar	dulār (m)	دولار
euro	yuru (m)	يورو
lira	lira iṭāliyya (f)	ليرة إيطالية
Deutschmark	mark almāniy (m)	مارك ألماني
franc	frank (m)	فرنك
pound sterling	ʒunayh istirlīniy (m)	جنيه استرليني
yen	yīn (m)	ين
debt	dayn (m)	دين
debtor	mudīn (m)	مدين
to lend (money)	sallaf	سلّف
to borrow (vi, vt)	istalaf	إستلف
bank	bank (m)	بنك
account	ḥisāb (m)	حساب
to deposit (vt)	awdaʿ	أودع
to deposit into the account	awdaʿ fil ḥisāb	أودع في الحساب
to withdraw (vt)	saḥab min al ḥisāb	سحب من الحساب
credit card	biṭāqat iʾtimān (f)	بطاقة إئتمان
cash	nuqūd (pl)	نقود
check	ʃīk (m)	شيك
to write a check	katab ʃīk	كتب شيكًا
checkbook	daftar ʃīkāt (m)	دفتر شيكات
wallet	maḥfaẓat ʒīb (f)	محفظة جيب
change purse	maḥfaẓat fakka (f)	محفظة فكّة
safe	xizāna (f)	خزانة
heir	wāris (m)	وارث
inheritance	wirāθa (f)	وراثة
fortune (wealth)	θarwa (f)	ثروة
lease	ʾīʒār (m)	إيجار
rent (money)	uʒrat as sakan (f)	أجرة السكن
to rent (sth from sb)	istaʾʒar	إستأجر
price	siʿr (m)	سعر

| cost | θaman (m) | ثمن |
| sum | mablaɣ (m) | مبلغ |

to spend (vt)	ṣaraf	صرف
expenses	maṣārīf (pl)	مصاريف
to economize (vi, vt)	waffar	وفّر
economical	muwaffir	موفّر

to pay (vi, vt)	dafa'	دفع
payment	daf' (m)	دفع
change (give the ~)	al bāqi (m)	الباقي

tax	ḍarība (f)	ضريبة
fine	ɣarāma (f)	غرامة
to fine (vt)	faraḍ ɣarāma	فرض غرامة

42. Post. Postal service

post office	maktab al barīd (m)	مكتب البريد
mail (letters, etc.)	al barīd (m)	البريد
mailman	sā'i al barīd (m)	ساعي البريد
opening hours	awqāt al 'amal (pl)	أوقات العمل

letter	risāla (f)	رسالة
registered letter	risāla musaȝȝala (f)	رسالة مسجّلة
postcard	biṭāqa barīdiyya (f)	بطاقة بريديّة
telegram	barqiyya (f)	برقيّة
package (parcel)	ṭard (m)	طرد
money transfer	ḥawāla māliyya (f)	حوالة ماليّة

to receive (vt)	istalam	إستلم
to send (vt)	arsal	أرسل
sending	irsāl (m)	إرسال
address	'unwān (m)	عنوان
ZIP code	raqm al barīd (m)	رقم البريد
sender	mursil (m)	مرسل
receiver	mursal ilayh (m)	مرسل إليه

| name (first name) | ism (m) | إسم |
| surname (last name) | ism al 'ā'ila (m) | إسم العائلة |

postage rate	ta'rīfa (f)	تعريفة
standard (adj)	'ādiy	عاديّ
economical (adj)	muwaffir	موفّر

weight	wazn (m)	وزن
to weigh (~ letters)	wazan	وزن
envelope	ẓarf (m)	ظرف
postage stamp	ṭābi' (m)	طابع
to stamp an envelope	alṣaq ṭābi'	ألصق طابعا

43. Banking

bank	bank (m)	بنك
branch (of bank, etc.)	far' (m)	فرع
bank clerk, consultant	muwazzaf bank (m)	موظف بنك
manager (director)	mudīr (m)	مدير
bank account	ḥisāb (m)	حساب
account number	raqm al ḥisāb (m)	رقم الحساب
checking account	ḥisāb ʒāri (m)	حساب جار
savings account	ḥisāb tawfīr (m)	حساب توفير
to open an account	fataḥ ḥisāb	فتح حسابا
to close the account	aɣlaq ḥisāb	أغلق حسابا
to deposit into the account	awda' fil ḥisāb	أودع في الحساب
to withdraw (vt)	saḥab min al ḥisāb	سحب من الحساب
deposit	wadī'a (f)	وديعة
to make a deposit	awda'	أودع
wire transfer	ḥawāla (f)	حوالة
to wire, to transfer	ḥawwal	حوّل
sum	mablaɣ (m)	مبلغ
How much?	kam?	كم؟
signature	tawqī' (m)	توقيع
to sign (vt)	waqqa'	وقّع
credit card	biṭāqat i'timān (f)	بطاقة ائتمان
code (PIN code)	kūd (m)	كود
credit card number	raqm biṭāqat i'timān (m)	رقم بطاقة إئتمان
ATM	ṣarrāf 'āliy (m)	صرّاف آلي
check	ʃīk (m)	شيك
to write a check	katab ʃīk	كتب شيكًا
checkbook	daftar ʃīkāt (m)	دفتر شيكات
loan (bank ~)	qarḍ (m)	قرض
to apply for a loan	qaddam ṭalab lil ḥuṣūl 'ala qarḍ	قدّم طلبا للحصول على قرض
to get a loan	ḥaṣal 'ala qarḍ	حصل على قرض
to give a loan	qaddam qarḍ	قدّم قرضا
guarantee	ḍamān (m)	ضمان

44. Telephone. Phone conversation

telephone	hātif (m)	هاتف
cell phone	hātif maḥmūl (m)	هاتف محمول

answering machine	muʒīb al hātif (m)	مجيب الهاتف
to call (by phone)	ittaṣal	إتّصل
phone call	mukālama tilifuniyya (f)	مكالمة تليفونية

to dial a number	ittaṣal bi raqm	إتّصل برقم
Hello!	alu!	ألو
to ask (vt)	sa'al	سأل
to answer (vi, vt)	radd	ردّ

to hear (vt)	samiʿ	سمع
well (adv)	ʒayyidan	جيّدًا
not well (adv)	sayyi'an	سيّئًا
noises (interference)	taʃwīʃ (m)	تشويش

receiver	sammāʿa (f)	سمّاعة
to pick up (~ the phone)	rafaʿ as sammāʿa	رفع السمّاعة
to hang up (~ the phone)	qafal as sammāʿa	قفل السمّاعة

busy (engaged)	maʃɣūl	مشغول
to ring (ab. phone)	rann	رنّ
telephone book	dalīl at tilifūn (m)	دليل التليفون

| local (adj) | maḥalliyya | ة محلّيّة |
| local call | mukālama hātifiyya maḥalliyya (f) | مكالمة هاتفيّة محلّيّة |

| long distance (~ call) | baʿīd al mada | بعيد المدى |
| long-distance call | mukālama baʿīdat al mada (f) | مكالمة بعيدة المدى |

| international (adj) | duwaliy | دوليّ |
| international call | mukālama duwaliyya (f) | مكالمة دوليّة |

45. Cell phone

cell phone	hātif maḥmūl (m)	هاتف محمول
display	ʒihāz ʿarḍ (m)	جهاز عرض
button	zirr (m)	زرّ
SIM card	sim kart (m)	سيم كارت

battery	baṭṭāriyya (f)	بطّاريّة
to be dead (battery)	xalaṣat	خلصت
charger	ʃāḥin (m)	شاحن

menu	qā'ima (f)	قائمة
settings	awḍāʿ (pl)	أوضاع
tune (melody)	naɣma (f)	نغمة
to select (vt)	ixtār	إختار

calculator	'āla ḥāsiba (f)	آلة حاسبة
voice mail	barīd ṣawtiy (m)	بريد صوتيّ
alarm clock	munabbih (m)	منبّه

contacts	ʒihāt al ittiṣāl (pl)	جهات الإتّصال
SMS (text message)	risāla qaṣīra ɛsɛmɛs (f)	رسالة قصيرة sms
subscriber	muʃtarik (m)	مشترك

46. Stationery

| ballpoint pen | qalam ʒāf (m) | قلم جاف |
| fountain pen | qalam rīʃa (m) | قلم ريشة |

pencil	qalam ruṣāṣ (m)	قلم رصاص
highlighter	markir (m)	ماركر
felt-tip pen	qalam χaṭṭāṭ (m)	قلم خطاط

| notepad | muðakkira (f) | مذكّرة |
| agenda (diary) | ʒadwal al aʕmāl (m) | جدول الأعمال |

ruler	masṭara (f)	مسطرة
calculator	'āla ḥāsiba (f)	آلة حاسبة
eraser	astīka (f)	استيكة
thumbtack	dabbūs (m)	دبّوس
paper clip	dabbūs waraq (m)	دبّوس ورق

glue	ṣamɣ (m)	صمغ
stapler	dabbāsa (f)	دبّاسة
hole punch	χarrāma (m)	خرّامة
pencil sharpener	mibrāt (f)	مبراة

47. Foreign languages

language	luɣa (f)	لغة
foreign (adj)	aʒnabiy	أجنبي
foreign language	luɣa aʒnabiyya (f)	لغة أجنبيّة
to study (vt)	daras	درس
to learn (language, etc.)	taʕallam	تعلّم

to read (vi, vt)	qara'	قرأ
to speak (vi, vt)	takallam	تكلّم
to understand (vt)	fahim	فهم
to write (vt)	katab	كتب

fast (adv)	bi surʕa	بسرعة
slowly (adv)	bi buṭ'	ببطء
fluently (adv)	bi ṭalāqa	بطلاقة

rules	qawāʕid (pl)	قواعد
grammar	an naḥw waṣ ṣarf (m)	النحو والصرف
vocabulary	mufradāt al luɣa (pl)	مفردات اللغة
phonetics	ṣawtīyyāt (pl)	صوتيّات

textbook	kitāb ta'līm (m)	كتاب تعليم
dictionary	qāmūs (m)	قاموس
teach-yourself book	kitāb ta'līm ðātiy (m)	كتاب تعليم ذاتيّ
phrasebook	kitāb lil 'ibārāt aʃʃā'i'a (m)	كتاب للعبارت الشائعة
cassette, tape	ʃarīṭ (m)	شريط
videotape	ʃarīṭ vidiyu (m)	شريط فيديو
CD, compact disc	si di (m)	سي دي
DVD	di vi di (m)	دي في دي
alphabet	alifbā' (m)	الفباء
to spell (vt)	tahaʒʒa	تهجّى
pronunciation	nuṭq (m)	نطق
accent	lukna (f)	لكنة
with an accent	bi lukna	بلكنة
without an accent	bi dūn lukna	بدون لكنة
word	kalima (f)	كلمة
meaning	ma'na (m)	معنى
course (e.g., a French ~)	dawra (f)	دورة
to sign up	saʒʒal ismahu	سجّل إسمه
teacher	mudarris (m)	مدرّس
translation (process)	tarʒama (f)	ترجمة
translation (text, etc.)	tarʒama (f)	ترجمة
translator	mutarʒim (m)	مترجم
interpreter	mutarʒim fawriy (m)	مترجم فوريّ
polyglot	'alīm bi 'iddat luɣāt (m)	عليم بعدّة لغات
memory	ðākira (f)	ذاكرة

T&P BOOKS

MEALS. RESTAURANT

48. Table setting
49. Restaurant
50. Meals
51. Cooked dishes
52. Food
53. Drinks
54. Vegetables
55. Fruits. Nuts
56. Bread. Candy
57. Spices

T&P Books Publishing

48. Table setting

spoon	mil'aqa (f)	ملعقة
knife	sikkīn (m)	سكّين
fork	ʃawka (f)	شوكة
cup (e.g., coffee ~)	finʒān (m)	فنجان
plate (dinner ~)	ṭabaq (m)	طبق
saucer	ṭabaq finʒān (m)	طبق فنجان
napkin (on table)	mandīl (m)	منديل
toothpick	xallat asnān (f)	خلّة أسنان

49. Restaurant

restaurant	maṭʿam (m)	مطعم
coffee house	kafé (m), maqha (m)	كافيه، مقهى
pub, bar	bār (m)	بار
tearoom	ṣālun ʃāy (m)	صالون شاي
waiter	nādil (m)	نادل
waitress	nādila (f)	نادلة
bartender	bārman (m)	بارمان
menu	qāʾimat aṭ ṭaʿām (f)	قائمة طعام
wine list	qāʾimat al xumūr (f)	قائمة خمور
to book a table	ḥaʒaz māʾida	حجز مائدة
course, dish	waʒba (f)	وجبة
to order (meal)	ṭalab	طلب
to make an order	ṭalab	طلب
aperitif	ʃarāb (m)	شراب
appetizer	muqabbilāt (pl)	مقبّلات
dessert	ḥalawiyyāt (pl)	حلويّات
check	ḥisāb (m)	حساب
to pay the check	dafaʿ al ḥisāb	دفع الحساب
to give change	aʿṭa al bāqi	أعطى الباقي
tip	baqʃīʃ (m)	بقشيش

50. Meals

food	akl (m)	أكل
to eat (vi, vt)	akal	أكل

breakfast	fuṭūr (m)	فطور
to have breakfast	afṭar	أفطر
lunch	ɣadā' (m)	غداء
to have lunch	taɣadda	تغدّى
dinner	'aʃā' (m)	عشاء
to have dinner	ta'aʃʃa	تعشّى

| appetite | ʃahiyya (f) | شهيّة |
| Enjoy your meal! | hanī'an marī'an! | إهنيئًا مريئًا |

to open (~ a bottle)	fataḥ	فتح
to spill (liquid)	dalaq	دلق
to spill out (vi)	indalaq	إندلق

to boil (vi)	ɣala	غلى
to boil (vt)	ɣala	غلى
boiled (~ water)	maɣliy	مغلي
to chill, cool down (vt)	barrad	برّد
to chill (vi)	tabarrad	تبرّد

| taste, flavor | ṭa'm (m) | طعم |
| aftertaste | al maðāq al 'āliq fil fam (m) | المذاق العالق فى الفم |

to slim down (lose weight)	faqad al wazn	فقد الوزن
diet	ḥimya ɣaðā'iyya (f)	حمية غذائية
vitamin	vitamīn (m)	فيتامين
calorie	su'ra ḥarāriyya (f)	سعرة حراريّة
vegetarian (n)	nabātiy (m)	نباتي
vegetarian (adj)	nabātiy	نباتي

fats (nutrient)	duhūn (pl)	دهون
proteins	brutināt (pl)	بروتينات
carbohydrates	naʃawiyyāt (pl)	نشويّات
slice (of lemon, ham)	ʃarīḥa (f)	شريحة
piece (of cake, pie)	qiṭ'a (f)	قطعة
crumb (of bread, cake, etc.)	futāta (f)	فتاتة

51. Cooked dishes

course, dish	waʒba (f)	وجبة
cuisine	maṭbaχ (m)	مطبخ
recipe	waṣfa (f)	وصفة
portion	waʒba (f)	وجبة

| salad | sulṭa (f) | سلطة |
| soup | ʃūrba (f) | شوربة |

| clear soup (broth) | maraq (m) | مرق |
| sandwich (bread) | sandawitʃ (m) | ساندويتش |

fried eggs	bayḍ maqliy (m)	بيض مقليّ
hamburger (beefburger)	hamburger (m)	هامبورجر
beefsteak	biftīk (m)	بفتيك

side dish	ṭabaq ʒānibiy (m)	طبق جانبيّ
spaghetti	spaɣitti (m)	سباغيتي
mashed potatoes	harīs baṭāṭis (m)	هريس بطاطس
pizza	bītza (f)	بيتزا
porridge (oatmeal, etc.)	ʿaṣīda (f)	عصيدة
omelet	bayḍ maxfūq (m)	بيض مخفوق

boiled (e.g., ~ beef)	maslūq	مسلوق
smoked (adj)	mudaxxin	مدخّن
fried (adj)	maqliy	مقليّ
dried (adj)	muʒaffaf	مجفّف
frozen (adj)	muʒammad	مجمّد
pickled (adj)	muxallil	مخلّل

sweet (sugary)	musakkar	مسكّر
salty (adj)	māliḥ	مالح
cold (adj)	bārid	بارد
hot (adj)	sāxin	ساخن
bitter (adj)	murr	مرّ
tasty (adj)	laðīð	لذيذ

to cook in boiling water	ṭabax	طبخ
to cook (dinner)	haḍḍar	حضّر
to fry (vt)	qala	قلي
to heat up (food)	saxxan	سخّن

to salt (vt)	mallaḥ	ملّح
to pepper (vt)	falfal	فلفل
to grate (vt)	baʃar	بشر
peel (n)	qiʃra (f)	قشرة
to peel (vt)	qaʃʃar	قشّر

52. Food

meat	laḥm (m)	لحم
chicken	daʒāʒ (m)	دجاج
Rock Cornish hen (poussin)	farrūʒ (m)	فرّوج
duck	baṭṭa (f)	بطّة
goose	iwazza (f)	إوزّة
game	ṣayd (m)	صيد
turkey	daʒāʒ rūmiy (m)	دجاج رومي

pork	laḥm al xinzīr (m)	لحم الخنزير
veal	laḥm il ʿiʒl (m)	لحم العجل
lamb	laḥm aḍ ḍa'n (m)	لحم الضأن

| beef | laḥm al baqar (m) | لحم البقر |
| rabbit | arnab (m) | أرنب |

sausage (bologna, pepperoni, etc.)	suʒuq (m)	سجق
vienna sausage (frankfurter)	suʒuq (m)	سجق
bacon	bikūn (m)	بيكون
ham	hām (m)	هام
gammon	faχð χinzīr (m)	فخذ خنزير

pâté	maʿʒūn laḥm (m)	معجون لحم
liver	kibda (f)	كبدة
hamburger (ground beef)	haʃwa (f)	حشوة
tongue	lisān (m)	لسان

egg	bayḍa (f)	بيضة
eggs	bayḍ (m)	بيض
egg white	bayāḍ al bayḍ (m)	بياض البيض
egg yolk	ṣafār al bayḍ (m)	صفار البيض

fish	samak (m)	سمك
seafood	fawākih al baḥr (pl)	فواكه البحر
caviar	kaviyār (m)	كافيار

crab	salṭaʿūn (m)	سلطعون
shrimp	ʒambari (m)	جمبري
oyster	maḥār (m)	محار
spiny lobster	karkand ʃāik (m)	كركند شائك
octopus	uχṭubūṭ (m)	أخطبوط
squid	kalmāri (m)	كالماري

sturgeon	samak al ḥaʃʃ (m)	سمك الحفش
salmon	salmūn (m)	سلمون
halibut	samak al halbūt (m)	سمك الهلبوت

cod	samak al qudd (m)	سمك القدّ
mackerel	usqumriy (m)	أسقمريّ
tuna	tūna (f)	تونة
eel	hankalīs (m)	حنكليس

trout	salmūn muraqqaṭ (m)	سلمون مرقّط
sardine	sardīn (m)	سردين
pike	samak al karāki (m)	سمك الكراكي
herring	rinʒa (f)	رنجة

bread	χubz (m)	خبز
cheese	ʒubna (f)	جبنة
sugar	sukkar (m)	سكّر
salt	milḥ (m)	ملح
rice	urz (m)	أرز
pasta (macaroni)	makarūna (f)	مكرونة

noodles	nūdlis (f)	نودلز
butter	zubda (f)	زبدة
vegetable oil	zayt (m)	زيت
sunflower oil	zayt 'abīd aʃ ʃams (m)	زيت عبيد الشمس
margarine	marɣarīn (m)	مرغرين

| olives | zaytūn (m) | زيتون |
| olive oil | zayt az zaytūn (m) | زيت الزيتون |

milk	ḥalīb (m)	حليب
condensed milk	ḥalīb mukaθθaf (m)	حليب مكثف
yogurt	yūɣurt (m)	يوغورت
sour cream	krīma ḥāmiḍa (f)	كريمة حامضة
cream (of milk)	krīma (f)	كريمة

| mayonnaise | mayunīz (m) | مايونيز |
| buttercream | krīmat zubda (f) | كريمة زبدة |

cereal grains (wheat, etc.)	ḥubūb (pl)	حبوب
flour	daqīq (m)	دقيق
canned food	mu'allabāt (pl)	معلبات

cornflakes	kurn fliks (m)	كورن فليكس
honey	'asal (m)	عسل
jam	murabba (m)	مربّى
chewing gum	'ilk (m)	علك

53. Drinks

water	mā' (m)	ماء
drinking water	mā' ʃurb (m)	ماء شرب
mineral water	mā' ma'daniy (m)	ماء معدنيّ

still (adj)	bi dūn ɣāz	بدون غاز
carbonated (adj)	mukarban	مكربن
sparkling (adj)	bil ɣāz	بالغاز
ice	θalӡ (m)	ثلج
with ice	biθ θalӡ	بالثلج

non-alcoholic (adj)	bi dūn kuḥūl	بدون كحول
soft drink	maʃrūb ɣāziy (m)	مشروب غازي
refreshing drink	maʃrūb muθallaӡ (m)	مشروب مثلج
lemonade	ʃarāb laymūn (m)	شراب ليمون

liquors	maʃrūbāt kuḥūliyya (pl)	مشروبات كحوليّة
wine	nabīð (f)	نبيذ
white wine	nibīð abyaḍ (m)	نبيذ أبيض
red wine	nabīð aḥmar (m)	نبيذ أحمر
liqueur	liqiūr (m)	ليكيور
champagne	ʃambāniya (f)	شمبانيا

vermouth	virmut (m)	فيرموث
whiskey	wiski (m)	وسكي
vodka	vudka (f)	فودكا
gin	ʒīn (m)	جين
cognac	kunyāk (m)	كونياك
rum	rum (m)	رم
coffee	qahwa (f)	قهوة
black coffee	qahwa sāda (f)	قهوة سادة
coffee with milk	qahwa bil ḥalīb (f)	قهوة بالحليب
cappuccino	kaputʃīnu (m)	كابتشينو
instant coffee	niskafi (m)	نيسكافيه
milk	ḥalīb (m)	حليب
cocktail	kuktayl (m)	كوكتيل
milkshake	milk ʃyk (m)	ميلك شيك
juice	ʿasīr (m)	عصير
tomato juice	ʿasīr ṭamāṭim (m)	عصير طماطم
orange juice	ʿasīr burtuqāl (m)	عصير برتقال
freshly squeezed juice	ʿasīr ṭāziʒ (m)	عصير طازج
beer	bīra (f)	بيرة
light beer	bīra xafīfa (f)	بيرة خفيفة
dark beer	bīra ɣāmiqa (f)	بيرة غامقة
tea	ʃāy (m)	شاي
black tea	ʃāy aswad (m)	شاي أسود
green tea	ʃāy axḍar (m)	شاي أخضر

54. Vegetables

vegetables	xuḍār (pl)	خضار
greens	xuḍrawāt waraqiyya (pl)	خضروات ورقيّة
tomato	ṭamāṭim (f)	طماطم
cucumber	xiyār (m)	خيار
carrot	ʒazar (m)	جزر
potato	baṭāṭis (f)	بطاطس
onion	baṣal (m)	بصل
garlic	θūm (m)	ثوم
cabbage	kurumb (m)	كرنب
cauliflower	qarnabīṭ (m)	قرنبيط
Brussels sprouts	kurumb brūksil (m)	كرنب بروكسل
broccoli	brukuli (m)	بركولي
beetroot	banʒar (m)	بنجر
eggplant	bātinʒān (m)	باذنجان
zucchini	kūsa (f)	كوسة

| pumpkin | qarʿ (m) | قرع |
| turnip | lift (m) | لفت |

parsley	baqdūnis (m)	بقدونس
dill	ʃabat (m)	شبت
lettuce	χass (m)	خسّ
celery	karafs (m)	كرفس
asparagus	halyūn (m)	هليون
spinach	sabāniχ (m)	سبانخ

pea	bisilla (f)	بسلّة
beans	fūl (m)	فول
corn (maize)	ðura (f)	ذرّة
kidney bean	faṣūliya (f)	فاصوليا

bell pepper	filfil (m)	فلفل
radish	fiʒl (m)	فجل
artichoke	χurʃūf (m)	خرشوف

55. Fruits. Nuts

fruit	fākiha (f)	فاكهة
apple	tuffāḥa (f)	تفّاحة
pear	kummaθra (f)	كمّثرى
lemon	laymūn (m)	ليمون
orange	burtuqāl (m)	برتقال
strawberry (garden ~)	farawla (f)	فراولة

mandarin	yūsufiy (m)	يوسفي
plum	barqūq (m)	برقوق
peach	durrāq (m)	دراق
apricot	miʃmiʃ (f)	مشمش
raspberry	tūt al ʿullayq al aḥmar (m)	توت العلّيق الأحمر
pineapple	ananās (m)	أناناس

banana	mawz (m)	موز
watermelon	baṭṭīχ aḥmar (m)	بطّيخ أحمر
grape	ʿinab (m)	عنب
cherry	karaz (m)	كرز
melon	baṭṭīχ aṣfar (f)	بطّيخ أصفر

grapefruit	zinbāʿ (m)	زنباع
avocado	avukādu (f)	أفوكاتو
papaya	babāya (m)	بابايا
mango	mangu (m)	مانجو
pomegranate	rummān (m)	رمان

| redcurrant | kiʃmiʃ aḥmar (m) | كشمش أحمر |
| blackcurrant | ʿinab aθ θaʿlab al aswad (m) | عنب الثعلب الأسود |

gooseberry	'inab aθ θa'lab (m)	عنب الثعلب
bilberry	'inab al aḥrāʒ (m)	عنب الأحراج
blackberry	θamar al 'ullayk (m)	ثمر العليق

raisin	zabīb (m)	زبيب
fig	tīn (m)	تين
date	tamr (m)	تمر

peanut	fūl sudāniy (m)	فول سودانيّ
almond	lawz (m)	لوز
walnut	'ayn al ʒamal (f)	عين الجمل
hazelnut	bunduq (m)	بندق
coconut	ʒawz al hind (m)	جوز هند
pistachios	fustuq (m)	فستق

56. Bread. Candy

bakers' confectionery (pastry)	ḥalawiyyāt (pl)	حلويَات
bread	xubz (m)	خبز
cookies	baskawīt (m)	بسكويت

chocolate (n)	ʃukulāta (f)	شكولاتة
chocolate (as adj)	biʃ ʃukulāta	بالشكولاتة
candy (wrapped)	bumbūn (m)	بونبون
cake (e.g., cupcake)	ka'k (m)	كعك
cake (e.g., birthday ~)	tūrta (f)	تورتة

| pie (e.g., apple ~) | fatīra (f) | فطيرة |
| filling (for cake, pie) | ḥaʃwa (f) | حشوة |

jam (whole fruit jam)	murabba (m)	مربَى
marmalade	marmalād (f)	مرملاد
waffles	wāfil (m)	وافل
ice-cream	muθallaʒāt (pl)	مثلَجات
pudding	būding (m)	بودنج

57. Spices

salt	milḥ (m)	ملح
salty (adj)	māliḥ	مالح
to salt (vt)	mallaḥ	ملَح

black pepper	filfil aswad (m)	فلفل أسود
red pepper (milled ~)	filfil aḥmar (m)	فلفل أحمر
mustard	ṣalṣat al xardal (f)	صلصة الخردل
horseradish	fiʒl ḥārr (m)	فجل حارّ
condiment	tābil (m)	تابل

spice	bahār (m)	بهار
sauce	ṣalṣa (f)	صلصة
vinegar	χall (m)	خلّ
anise	yānsūn (m)	يانسون
basil	rīḥān (m)	ريحان
cloves	qurumful (m)	قرنفل
ginger	zanʒabīl (m)	زنجبيل
coriander	kuzbara (f)	كزبرة
cinnamon	qirfa (f)	قرفة
sesame	simsim (m)	سمسم
bay leaf	awrāq al γār (pl)	أوراق الغار
paprika	babrika (f)	بابريكا
caraway	karāwiya (f)	كراوية
saffron	zaʿfarān (m)	زعفران

PERSONAL INFORMATION. FAMILY

58. Personal information. Forms
59. Family members. Relatives
60. Friends. Coworkers

T&P Books Publishing

58. Personal information. Forms

name (first name)	ism (m)	إسم
surname (last name)	ism al 'ā'ila (m)	إسم العائلة
date of birth	tarīx al mīlād (m)	تاريخ الميلاد
place of birth	makān al mīlād (m)	مكان الميلاد
nationality	ʒinsiyya (f)	جنسية
place of residence	maqarr al iqāma (m)	مقر الإقامة
country	balad (m)	بلد
profession (occupation)	mihna (f)	مهنة
gender, sex	ʒins (m)	جنس
height	ṭūl (m)	طول
weight	wazn (m)	وزن

59. Family members. Relatives

mother	umm (f)	أمّ
father	ab (m)	أب
son	ibn (m)	إبن
daughter	ibna (f)	إبنة
younger daughter	al ibna aṣ ṣaɣīra (f)	الإبنة الصغيرة
younger son	al ibn aṣ ṣaɣīr (m)	الابن الصغير
eldest daughter	al ibna al kabīra (f)	الإبنة الكبيرة
eldest son	al ibn al kabīr (m)	الإبن الكبير
brother	ax (m)	أخ
elder brother	al ax al kabīr (m)	الأخ الكبير
younger brother	al ax aṣ ṣaɣīr (m)	الأخ الصغير
sister	uxt (f)	أخت
elder sister	al uxt al kabīra (f)	الأخت الكبيرة
younger sister	al uxt aṣ ṣaɣīra (f)	الأخت الصغيرة
cousin (masc.)	ibn 'amm (m), ibn xāl (m)	إبن عمّ، إبن خال
cousin (fem.)	ibnat 'amm (f), ibnat xāl (f)	إبنة عمّ، إبنة خال
mom, mommy	mama (f)	ماما
dad, daddy	baba (m)	بابا
parents	wālidān (du)	والدان
child	ṭifl (m)	طفل
children	aṭfāl (pl)	أطفال
grandmother	ʒidda (f)	جدّة
grandfather	ʒadd (m)	جدّ

grandson	ḥafīd (m)	حفيد
granddaughter	ḥafīda (f)	حفيدة
grandchildren	aḥfād (pl)	أحفاد

uncle	'amm (m), χāl (m)	عمّ, خال
aunt	'amma (f), χāla (f)	عمّة, خالة
nephew	ibn al aχ (m), ibn al uχt (m)	إبن الأخ, إبن الأخت
niece	ibnat al aχ (f), ibnat al uχt (f)	إبنة الأخ, إبنة الأخت
mother-in-law (wife's mother)	ḥamātt (f)	حماة

| father-in-law (husband's father) | ḥamm (m) | حم |

| son-in-law (daughter's husband) | zawʒ al ibna (m) | زوج الأبنة |

| stepmother | zawʒat al ab (f) | زوجة الأب |
| stepfather | zawʒ al umm (m) | زوج الأمّ |

infant	ṭifl raḍī' (m)	طفل رضيع
baby (infant)	mawlūd (m)	مولود
little boy, kid	walad ṣaɣīr (m)	ولد صغير

wife	zawʒa (f)	زوجة
husband	zawʒ (m)	زوج
spouse (husband)	zawʒ (m)	زوج
spouse (wife)	zawʒa (f)	زوجة

married (masc.)	mutazawwiʒ	متزوّج
married (fem.)	mutazawwiʒa	متزوّجة
single (unmarried)	a'zab	أعزب
bachelor	a'zab (m)	أعزب
divorced (masc.)	muṭallaq (m)	مطلّق
widow	armala (f)	أرملة
widower	armal (m)	أرمل

relative	qarīb (m)	قريب
close relative	nasīb qarīb (m)	نسيب قريب
distant relative	nasīb ba'īd (m)	نسيب بعيد
relatives	aqārib (pl)	أقارب

orphan (boy or girl)	yatīm (m)	يتيم
guardian (of a minor)	waliyy amr (m)	ولي أمر
to adopt (a boy)	tabanna	تبنّى
to adopt (a girl)	tabanna	تبنّى

60. Friends. Coworkers

friend (masc.)	ṣadīq (m)	صديق
friend (fem.)	ṣadīqa (f)	صديقة
friendship	ṣadāqa (f)	صداقة
to be friends	ṣādaq	صادق

buddy (masc.)	ṣāḥib (m)	صاحب
buddy (fem.)	ṣaḥiba (f)	صاحبة
partner	rafīq (m)	رفيق
chief (boss)	raʾīs (m)	رئيس
superior (n)	raʾīs (m)	رئيس
owner, proprietor	ṣāḥib (m)	صاحب
subordinate (n)	tābiʿ (m)	تابع
colleague	zamīl (m)	زميل
acquaintance (person)	maʿruf (m)	معروف
fellow traveler	rafīq safar (m)	رفيق سفر
classmate	zamīl fiṣ ṣaff (m)	زميل في الصفَ
neighbor (masc.)	ʒār (m)	جار
neighbor (fem.)	ʒāra (f)	جارة
neighbors	ʒirān (pl)	جيران

T&P BOOKS

HUMAN BODY.
MEDICINE

61. Head
62. Human body
63. Diseases
64. Symptoms. Treatments. Part 1
65. Symptoms. Treatments. Part 2
66. Symptoms. Treatments. Part 3
67. Medicine. Drugs. Accessories

T&P Books Publishing

61. Head

head	ra's (m)	رأس
face	waʒh (m)	وجه
nose	anf (m)	أنف
mouth	fam (m)	فم
eye	ʿayn (f)	عين
eyes	ʿuyūn (pl)	عيون
pupil	ḥadaqa (f)	حدقة
eyebrow	ḥāʒib (m)	حاجب
eyelash	rimʃ (m)	رمش
eyelid	ʒafn (m)	جفن
tongue	lisān (m)	لسان
tooth	sinn (f)	سن
lips	ʃifāh (pl)	شفاه
cheekbones	ʿiẓām waʒhiyya (pl)	عظام وجهيّة
gum	liθθa (f)	لثّة
palate	ḥanak (m)	حنك
nostrils	minxarān (du)	منخران
chin	ðaqan (m)	ذقن
jaw	fakk (m)	فكّ
cheek	xadd (m)	خدّ
forehead	ʒabha (f)	جبهة
temple	ṣudɣ (m)	صدغ
ear	uðun (f)	أذن
back of the head	qafa (m)	قفا
neck	raqaba (f)	رقبة
throat	ḥalq (m)	حلق
hair	ʃaʿr (m)	شعر
hairstyle	tasrīḥa (f)	تسريحة
haircut	tasrīḥa (f)	تسريحة
wig	barūka (f)	باروكة
mustache	ʃawārib (pl)	شوارب
beard	liḥya (f)	لحية
to have (a beard, etc.)	ʿindahu	عنده
braid	ḍifīra (f)	ضفيرة
sideburns	sawālif (pl)	سوالف
red-haired (adj)	aḥmar aʃʃaʿr	أحمر الشعر
gray (hair)	abyaḍ	أبيض

bald (adj)	aṣlaʿ	أصلع
bald patch	ṣalaʿ (m)	صلع
ponytail	ðayl ḥiṣān (m)	ذيل حصان
bangs	quṣṣa (f)	قصّة

62. Human body

hand	yad (m)	يد
arm	ðirāʿ (f)	ذراع
finger	iṣbaʿ (m)	إصبع
toe	iṣbaʿ al qadam (m)	إصبع القدم
thumb	ibhām (m)	إبهام
little finger	ҳunṣur (m)	خنصر
nail	ẓufr (m)	ظفر
fist	qabḍa (f)	قبضة
palm	kaff (f)	كفّ
wrist	miʿṣam (m)	معصم
forearm	sāʿid (m)	ساعد
elbow	mirfaq (m)	مرفق
shoulder	katf (f)	كتف
leg	riʒl (f)	رجل
foot	qadam (f)	قدم
knee	rukba (f)	ركبة
calf (part of leg)	sammāna (f)	سمّانة
hip	faҳð (f)	فخذ
heel	ʿaqb (m)	عقب
body	ʒism (m)	جسم
stomach	baṭn (m)	بطن
chest	ṣadr (m)	صدر
breast	θady (m)	ثدي
flank	ʒamb (m)	جنب
back	ẓahr (m)	ظهر
lower back	asfal aẓ ẓahr (m)	أسفل الظهر
waist	ҳaṣr (m)	خصر
navel (belly button)	surra (f)	سرّة
buttocks	ardāf (pl)	أرداف
bottom	dubr (m)	دبر
beauty mark	ʃāma (f)	شامة
birthmark	waḥma	وحمة
(café au lait spot)		
tattoo	waʃm (m)	وشم
scar	nadba (f)	ندبة

63. Diseases

sickness	maraḍ (m)	مرض
to be sick	maraḍ	مرض
health	ṣiḥḥa (f)	صحّة
runny nose (coryza)	zukām (m)	زكام
tonsillitis	iltihāb al lawzatayn (m)	التهاب اللوزتين
cold (illness)	bard (m)	برد
to catch a cold	aṣābahu al bard	أصابه البرد
bronchitis	iltihāb al qaṣabāt (m)	إلتهاب القصبات
pneumonia	iltihāb ar ri'atayn (m)	إلتهاب الرئتين
flu, influenza	inflūnza (f)	إنفلونزا
nearsighted (adj)	qaṣīr an naẓar	قصير النظر
farsighted (adj)	ba'īd an naẓar	بعيد النظر
strabismus (crossed eyes)	ḥawal (m)	حول
cross-eyed (adj)	aḥwal	أحول
cataract	katarakt (f)	كاتاراكت
glaucoma	glawkūma (f)	جلوكوما
stroke	sakta (f)	سكتة
heart attack	iḥtiʃā' (m)	إحتشاء
myocardial infarction	nawba qalbiya (f)	نوبة قلبية
paralysis	ʃalal (m)	شلل
to paralyze (vt)	ʃall	شلّ
allergy	ḥassāsiyya (f)	حسّاسيّة
asthma	rabw (m)	ربو
diabetes	ad dā' as sukkariy (m)	الداء السكّريّ
toothache	alam al asnān (m)	ألم الأسنان
caries	naχar al asnān (m)	نخر الأسنان
diarrhea	ishāl (m)	إسهال
constipation	imsāk (m)	إمساك
stomach upset	'usr al haḍm (m)	عسر الهضم
food poisoning	tasammum (m)	تسمّم
to get food poisoning	tasammam	تسمّم
arthritis	iltihāb al mafāṣil (m)	إلتهاب المفاصل
rickets	kusāḥ al aṭfāl (m)	كساح الأطفال
rheumatism	riumatizm (m)	روماتزم
atherosclerosis	taṣṣallub aʃ ʃarayīn (m)	تصلّب الشرايين
gastritis	iltihāb al ma'ida (m)	إلتهاب المعدة
appendicitis	iltihāb az zā'ida ad dūdiyya (m)	إلتهاب الزائدة الدوديّة
cholecystitis	iltihāb al marāra (m)	إلتهاب المرارة
ulcer	qurḥa (f)	قرحة

measles	maraḍ al ḥaṣba (m)	مرض الحصبة
rubella (German measles)	ḥaṣba almāniyya (f)	حصبة ألمانية
jaundice	yaraqān (m)	يرقان
hepatitis	iltihāb al kabd al vayrūsiy (m)	إلتهاب الكبد الفيروسيّ
schizophrenia	ʃizufrīniya (f)	شيزوفرينيا
rabies (hydrophobia)	dāʾ al kalb (m)	داء الكلب
neurosis	ʿiṣāb (m)	عصاب
concussion	irtiʒāʒ al muxx (m)	إرتجاج المخ
cancer	saraṭān (m)	سرطان
sclerosis	taṣṣallub (m)	تصلب
multiple sclerosis	taṣṣallub mutaʿaddid (m)	تصلب متعدد
alcoholism	idmān al xamr (m)	إدمان الخمر
alcoholic (n)	mudmin al xamr (m)	مدمن الخمر
syphilis	sifilis az zuhariy (m)	سفلس الزهري
AIDS	al aydz (m)	الايدز
tumor	waram (m)	ورم
malignant (adj)	xabīθ	خبيث
benign (adj)	ḥamīd (m)	حميد
fever	ḥumma (f)	حمّى
malaria	malāriya (f)	ملاريا
gangrene	ɣanɣrīna (f)	غنفرينا
seasickness	duwār al baḥr (m)	دوار البحر
epilepsy	maraḍ aṣ ṣarʿ (m)	مرض الصرع
epidemic	wabāʾ (m)	وباء
typhus	tīfus (m)	تيفوس
tuberculosis	maraḍ as sull (m)	مرض السلّ
cholera	kulīra (f)	كوليرا
plague (bubonic ~)	ṭāʿūn (m)	طاعون

64. Symptoms. Treatments. Part 1

symptom	ʿaraḍ (m)	عرض
temperature	ḥarāra (f)	حرارة
high temperature (fever)	ḥumma (f)	حمّى
pulse	nabḍ (m)	نبض
dizziness (vertigo)	dawxa (f)	دوخة
hot (adj)	ḥārr	حارّ
shivering	nafaḍān (m)	نفضان
pale (e.g., ~ face)	aṣfar	أصفر
cough	suʿāl (m)	سعال
to cough (vi)	saʿal	سعل

to sneeze (vi)	ʿaṭas	عطس
faint	iɣmāʾ (m)	إغماء
to faint (vi)	ɣumiya ʿalayh	غمي عليه

bruise (hématome)	kadma (f)	كَدمة
bump (lump)	tawarrum (m)	تورّم
to bang (bump)	iṣṭadam	إصطدم
contusion (bruise)	raḍḍ (m)	رضّ
to get a bruise	taraḍḍaḍ	ترضّض

to limp (vi)	ʿaraʒ	عرج
dislocation	χalʿ (m)	خلع
to dislocate (vt)	χalaʿ	خلع
fracture	kasr (m)	كسر
to have a fracture	inkasar	إنكسر

cut (e.g., paper ~)	ʒurḥ (m)	جرح
to cut oneself	ʒaraḥ nafsah	جرح نفسه
bleeding	nazf (m)	نزف

| burn (injury) | ḥarq (m) | حرق |
| to get burned | taʃayyat | تشيّط |

to prick (vt)	waχaz	وخز
to prick oneself	waχaz nafsah	وخز نفسه
to injure (vt)	aṣāb	أصاب
injury	iṣāba (f)	إصابة
wound	ʒurḥ (m)	جرح
trauma	ṣadma (f)	صدمة

to be delirious	haða	هذى
to stutter (vi)	talaʿsam	تلعثم
sunstroke	ḍarbat ʃams (f)	ضربة شمس

65. Symptoms. Treatments. Part 2

| pain, ache | alam (m) | ألم |
| splinter (in foot, etc.) | ʃaẓiyya (f) | شظيّة |

sweat (perspiration)	ʿirq (m)	عرق
to sweat (perspire)	ʿariq	عرق
vomiting	taqayyuʿ (m)	تقيؤ
convulsions	taʃannuʒāt (pl)	تشنّجات

pregnant (adj)	ḥāmil	حامل
to be born	wulid	وُلد
delivery, labor	wilāda (f)	ولادة
to deliver (~ a baby)	walad	ولد
abortion	iʒhāḍ (m)	إجهاض
breathing, respiration	tanaffus (m)	تنفّس

in-breath (inhalation)	istinʃāq (m)	إستنشاق
out-breath (exhalation)	zafīr (m)	زفير
to exhale (breathe out)	zafar	زفر
to inhale (vi)	istanʃaq	إستنشق

disabled person	muʿāq (m)	معاق
cripple	muqʿad (m)	مقعد
drug addict	mudmin muxaddirāt (m)	مدمن مخدّرات

deaf (adj)	aṭraʃ	أطرش
mute (adj)	axras	أخرس
deaf mute (adj)	aṭraʃ axras	أطرش أخرس

mad, insane (adj)	maʒnūn (m)	مجنون
madman (demented person)	maʒnūn (m)	مجنون
madwoman	maʒnūna (f)	مجنونة
to go insane	ʒunn	جنّ

gene	ʒīn (m)	جين
immunity	manāʿa (f)	مناعة
hereditary (adj)	wirāθiy	وراثيّ
congenital (adj)	xilqiy munð al wilāda	خلقيّ منذ الولادة

virus	virūs (m)	فيروس
microbe	mikrūb (m)	ميكروب
bacterium	ʒurθūma (f)	جرثومة
infection	ʿadwa (f)	عدوى

66. Symptoms. Treatments. Part 3

| hospital | mustaʃfa (m) | مستشفى |
| patient | marīḍ (m) | مريض |

diagnosis	taʃxīṣ (m)	تشخيص
cure	ʿilāʒ (m)	علاج
medical treatment	ʿilāʒ (m)	علاج
to get treatment	taʿālaʒ	تعالج
to treat (~ a patient)	ʿālaʒ	عالج
to nurse (look after)	marraḍ	مرّض
care (nursing ~)	ʿināya (f)	عناية

operation, surgery	ʿamaliyya ʒarahiyya (f)	عمليّة جرحيّة
to bandage (head, limb)	ḍammad	ضمّد
bandaging	taḍmīd (m)	تضميد

vaccination	talqīḥ (m)	تلقيح
to vaccinate (vt)	laqqaḥ	لقّح
injection, shot	ḥuqna (f)	حقنة
to give an injection	ḥaqan ibra	حقن إبرة

attack	nawba (f)	نوبة
amputation	batr (m)	بتر
to amputate (vt)	batar	بتر
coma	ɣaybūba (f)	غيبوبة
to be in a coma	kān fi ḥālat ɣaybūba	كان في حالة غيبوبة
intensive care	al 'ināya al murakkaza (f)	العناية المركزة

to recover (~ from flu)	ʃufiy	شفي
condition (patient's ~)	ḥāla (f)	حالة
consciousness	wa'y (m)	وعي
memory (faculty)	ðākira (f)	ذاكرة

to pull out (tooth)	χala'	خلع
filling	haʃw (m)	حشو
to fill (a tooth)	haʃa	حشا

| hypnosis | at tanwīm al maɣnaṭīsiy (m) | التنويم المغناطيسيّ |
| to hypnotize (vt) | nawwam | نوّم |

67. Medicine. Drugs. Accessories

medicine, drug	dawā' (m)	دواء
remedy	'ilāʒ (m)	علاج
to prescribe (vt)	waṣaf	وصف
prescription	waṣfa (f)	وصفة

tablet, pill	qurṣ (m)	قرص
ointment	marham (m)	مرهم
ampule	ambūla (f)	أمبولة
mixture	dawā' ʃarāb (m)	دواء شراب
syrup	ʃarāb (m)	شراب
pill	ḥabba (f)	حبّة
powder	ðarūr (m)	ذرور

gauze bandage	ḍammāda (f)	ضمادة
cotton wool	quṭn (m)	قطن
iodine	yūd (m)	يود
Band-Aid	blāstir (m)	بلاستر
eyedropper	māṣṣat al bastara (f)	ماصّة البسترة
thermometer	tirmūmitr (m)	ترمومتر
syringe	mihqana (f)	محقنة

| wheelchair | kursiy mutaḥarrik (m) | كرسي متحرّك |
| crutches | 'ukkāzān (du) | عكّازان |

painkiller	musakkin (m)	مسكّن
laxative	mulayyin (m)	مليّن
spirits (ethanol)	iθanūl (m)	إيثانول
medicinal herbs	a'ʃāb ṭibbiyya (pl)	أعشاب طبية
herbal (~ tea)	'uʃbiy	عشبيّ

T&P BOOKS

APARTMENT

68. Apartment
69. Furniture. Interior
70. Bedding
71. Kitchen
72. Bathroom
73. Household appliances

T&P Books Publishing

68. Apartment

apartment	ʃaqqa (f)	شقّة
room	ɣurfa (f)	غرفة
bedroom	ɣurfat an nawm (f)	غرفة النوم
dining room	ɣurfat il akl (f)	غرفة الأكل
living room	ṣālat al istiqbāl (f)	صالة الإستقبال
study (home office)	maktab (m)	مكتب

entry room	madχal (m)	مدخل
bathroom (room with a bath or shower)	ḥammām (m)	حمّام
half bath	ḥammām (m)	حمّام

ceiling	saqf (m)	سقف
floor	arḍ (f)	أرض
corner	zāwiya (f)	زاوية

69. Furniture. Interior

furniture	aθāθ (m)	أثاث
table	maktab (m)	مكتب
chair	kursiy (m)	كرسيّ
bed	sarīr (m)	سرير
couch, sofa	kanaba (f)	كنبة
armchair	kursiy (m)	كرسيّ

| bookcase | χizānat kutub (f) | خزانة كتب |
| shelf | raff (m) | رفّ |

wardrobe	dūlāb (m)	دولاب
coat rack (wall-mounted ~)	ʃammā'a (f)	شمّاعة
coat stand	ʃammā'a (f)	شمّاعة

| bureau, dresser | dulāb adrāʒ (m) | دولاب أدراج |
| coffee table | ṭāwilat al qahwa (f) | طاولة القهوة |

mirror	mir'āt (f)	مرآة
carpet	siʒāda (f)	سجادة
rug, small carpet	siʒāda (f)	سجادة

fireplace	midfa'a ḥā'iṭiyya (f)	مدفأة حائطيّة
candle	ʃam'a (f)	شمعة
candlestick	ʃam'adān (m)	شمعدان

drapes	satā'ir (pl)	ستائر
wallpaper	waraq ḥī'ṭān (m)	ورق حيطان
blinds (jalousie)	haṣīrat ʃubbāk (f)	حصيرة شبّاك

table lamp	miṣbāḥ aṭ ṭāwila (m)	مصباح الطاولة
wall lamp (sconce)	miṣbāḥ al ḥā'iṭ (f)	مصباح الحائط
floor lamp	miṣbāḥ arḍiy (m)	مصباح أرضيّ
chandelier	naʒafa (f)	نجفة

leg (of chair, table)	riʒl (f)	رجل
armrest	masnad (m)	مسند
back (backrest)	masnad (m)	مسند
drawer	durʒ (m)	درج

70. Bedding

bedclothes	bayāḍāt as sarīr (pl)	بياضات السرير
pillow	wisāda (f)	وسادة
pillowcase	kīs al wisāda (m)	كيس الوسادة
duvet, comforter	baṭṭāniyya (f)	بطّانيّة
sheet	milāya (f)	ملاية
bedspread	ɣiṭā' as sarīr (m)	غطاء السرير

71. Kitchen

kitchen	maṭbax (m)	مطبخ
gas	ɣāz (m)	غاز
gas stove (range)	butuɣāz (m)	بوتوغاز
electric stove	furn kaharabā'iy (m)	فرن كهربائيّ
oven	furn (m)	فرن
microwave oven	furn al mikruwayv (m)	فرن الميكروويف

refrigerator	θallāʒa (f)	ثلاجة
freezer	frīzir (m)	فريزر
dishwasher	ɣassāla (f)	غسّالة

meat grinder	farrāmat laḥm (f)	فرّامة لحم
juicer	'aṣṣāra (f)	عصّارة
toaster	maḥmaṣat xubz (f)	محمصة خبز
mixer	xallāṭ (m)	خلّاط

coffee machine	mākinat ṣan' al qahwa (f)	ماكينة صنع القهوة
coffee pot	kanaka (f)	كنكة
coffee grinder	maṭḥanat qahwa (f)	مطحنة قهوة

kettle	barrād (m)	برّاد
teapot	barrād aʃ ʃāy (m)	برّاد الشاي
lid	ɣiṭā' (m)	غطاء

tea strainer	miṣfāt (f)	مصفاة
spoon	mil'aqa (f)	ملعقة
teaspoon	mil'aqat ʃāy (f)	ملعقة شاي
soup spoon	mil'aqa kabīra (f)	ملعقة كبيرة
fork	ʃawka (f)	شوكة
knife	sikkīn (m)	سكّين

tableware (dishes)	ṣuḥūn (pl)	صحون
plate (dinner ~)	ṭabaq (m)	طبق
saucer	ṭabaq finʒān (m)	طبق فنجان

shot glass	ka's (f)	كأس
glass (tumbler)	kubbāya (f)	كبّاية
cup	finʒān (m)	فنجان

sugar bowl	sukkariyya (f)	سكّريّة
salt shaker	mamlaḥa (f)	مملحة
pepper shaker	mabhara (f)	مبهرة
butter dish	ṣuḥn zubda (m)	صحن زبدة

stock pot (soup pot)	kassirūlla (f)	كاسرولة
frying pan (skillet)	ṭāsa (f)	طاسة
ladle	miɣrafa (f)	مغرفة
colander	miṣfāt (f)	مصفاة
tray (serving ~)	ṣīniyya (f)	صينيّة

bottle	zuʒāʒa (f)	زجاجة
jar (glass)	barṭamān (m)	برطمان
can	tanaka (f)	تنكة

bottle opener	fattāḥa (f)	فتّاحة
can opener	fattāḥa (f)	فتّاحة
corkscrew	barrīma (f)	بريمة
filter	filtir (m)	فلتر
to filter (vt)	ṣaffa	صفّى

| trash, garbage (food waste, etc.) | zubāla (f) | زبالة |
| trash can (kitchen ~) | ṣundūq az zubāla (m) | صندوق الزبالة |

72. Bathroom

bathroom	ḥammām (m)	حمّام
water	mā' (m)	ماء
faucet	ḥanafiyya (f)	حنفيّة
hot water	mā' sāxin (m)	ماء ساخن
cold water	mā' bārid (m)	ماء بارد

| toothpaste | ma'ʒūn asnān (m) | معجون أسنان |
| to brush one's teeth | naẓẓaf al asnān | نظّف الأسنان |

toothbrush	furʃat asnān (f)	فرشة أسنان
to shave (vi)	ḥalaq	حلق
shaving foam	raɣwa lil ḥilāqa (f)	رغوة للحلاقة
razor	mūs ḥilāqa (m)	موس حلاقة

to wash (one's hands, etc.)	ɣasal	غسل
to take a bath	istaḥamm	إستحمّ
shower	dūʃ (m)	دوش
to take a shower	axað ad duʃ	أخذ الدش

bathtub	ḥawḍ istiḥmām (m)	حوض استحمام
toilet (toilet bowl)	mirḥāḍ (m)	مرحاض
sink (washbasin)	ḥawḍ (m)	حوض

| soap | ṣābūn (m) | صابون |
| soap dish | ṣabbāna (f) | صبّانة |

sponge	līfa (f)	ليفة
shampoo	ʃāmbū (m)	شامبو
towel	fūṭa (f)	فوطة
bathrobe	θawb ḥammām (m)	ثوب حمّام

laundry (process)	ɣasīl (m)	غسيل
washing machine	ɣassāla (f)	غسّالة
to do the laundry	ɣasal al malābis	غسل الملابس
laundry detergent	mashūq ɣasīl (m)	مسحوق غسيل

73. Household appliances

TV set	tilivizyūn (m)	تليفزيون
tape recorder	ʒihāz tasʒīl (m)	جهاز تسجيل
VCR (video recorder)	ʒihāz tasʒīl vidiyu (m)	جهاز تسجيل فيديو
radio	ʒihāz radiyu (m)	جهاز راديو
player (CD, MP3, etc.)	blayir (m)	بلاير

video projector	'āriḍ vidiyu (m)	عارض فيديو
home movie theater	sinima manziliyya (f)	سينما منزليّة
DVD player	di vi di (m)	دي في دي
amplifier	mukabbir aṣ ṣawt (m)	مكبّر الصوت
video game console	'atāri (m)	أتاري

video camera	kamira vidiyu (f)	كاميرا فيديو
camera (photo)	kamira (f)	كاميرا
digital camera	kamira diʒital (f)	كاميرا ديجيتال

vacuum cleaner	miknasa kahrabā'iyya (f)	مكنسة كهربائيّة
iron (e.g., steam ~)	makwāt (f)	مكواة
ironing board	lawḥat kayy (f)	لوحة كيّ
telephone	hātif (m)	هاتف
cell phone	hātif maḥmūl (m)	هاتف محمول

| typewriter | 'āla katiba (f) | آلة كاتبة |
| sewing machine | 'ālat al χiyāṭa (f) | آلة الخياطة |

microphone	mikrufūn (m)	ميكروفون
headphones	sammā'āt ra'siya (pl)	سمّاعات رأسيّة
remote control (TV)	rimuwt kuntrūl (m)	ريموت كنترول

CD, compact disc	si di (m)	سي دي
cassette, tape	ʃarīṭ (m)	شريط
vinyl record	usṭuwāna (f)	أسطوانة

THE EARTH. WEATHER

74. Outer space
75. The Earth
76. Cardinal directions
77. Sea. Ocean
78. Seas' and Oceans' names
79. Mountains
80. Mountains names
81. Rivers
82. Rivers' names
83. Forest
84. Natural resources
85. Weather
86. Severe weather. Natural disasters

T&P Books Publishing

space	faḍā' (m)	فضاء
space (as adj)	faḍā'iy	فضائيّ
outer space	faḍā' (m)	فضاء
world	'ālam (m)	عالم
universe	al kawn (m)	الكون
galaxy	al maʒarra (f)	المجرّة
star	naʒm (m)	نجم
constellation	burʒ (m)	برج
planet	kawkab (m)	كوكب
satellite	qamar ṣinā'iy (m)	قمر صناعيّ
meteorite	ḥaʒar nayzakiy (m)	حجر نيزكيّ
comet	muðannab (m)	مذنّب
asteroid	kuwaykib (m)	كويكب
orbit	madār (m)	مدار
to revolve (~ around the Earth)	dār	دار
atmosphere	al ɣilāf al ʒawwiy (m)	الغلاف الجويّ
the Sun	aʃʃams (f)	الشمس
solar system	al maʒmū'a aʃʃamsiyya (f)	المجموعة الشمسيّة
solar eclipse	kusūf aʃʃams (m)	كسوف الشمس
the Earth	al arḍ (f)	الأرض
the Moon	al qamar (m)	القمر
Mars	al mirrīχ (m)	المرّيخ
Venus	az zahra (f)	الزهرة
Jupiter	al muʃtari (m)	المشتري
Saturn	zuḥal (m)	زحل
Mercury	'aṭārid (m)	عطارد
Uranus	urānus (m)	اورانوس
Neptune	nibtūn (m)	نبتون
Pluto	blūtu (m)	بلوتو
Milky Way	darb at tabbāna (m)	درب التبّانة
Great Bear (Ursa Major)	ad dubb al akbar (m)	الدبّ الأكبر
North Star	naʒm al 'qutb (m)	نجم القطب
Martian	sākin al mirrīχ (m)	ساكن المرّيخ
extraterrestrial (n)	faḍā'iy (m)	فضائيّ

alien	faḍā'iy (m)	فضائيّ
flying saucer	ṭabaq ṭā'ir (m)	طبق طائر
spaceship	markaba faḍā'iyya (f)	مركبة فضائيّة
space station	maḥaṭṭat faḍā' (f)	محطّة فضاء
blast-off	intilāq (m)	إنطلاق
engine	mutūr (m)	موتور
nozzle	manfaθ (m)	منفث
fuel	wuqūd (m)	وقود
cockpit, flight deck	kabīna (f)	كابينة
antenna	hawā'iy (m)	هوائيّ
porthole	kuwwa mustadīra (f)	كوّة مستديرة
solar panel	lawḥ ʃamsiy (m)	لوح شمسيّ
spacesuit	baðlat al faḍā' (f)	بذلة الفضاء
weightlessness	in'idām al wazn (m)	إنعدام الوزن
oxygen	uksiʒīn (m)	أكسجين
docking (in space)	rasw (m)	رسو
to dock (vi, vt)	rasa	رسا
observatory	marṣad (m)	مرصد
telescope	tiliskūp (m)	تلسكوب
to observe (vt)	rāqab	راقب
to explore (vt)	istakʃaf	إستكشف

75. The Earth

the Earth	al arḍ (f)	الأرض
the globe (the Earth)	al kura al arḍiyya (f)	الكرة الأرضيّة
planet	kawkab (m)	كوكب
atmosphere	al yilāf al ʒawwiy (m)	الغلاف الجوّيّ
geography	ʒuyrāfiya (f)	جغرافيا
nature	ṭabī'a (f)	طبيعة
globe (table ~)	namūðaʒ lil kura al arḍiyya (m)	نموذج للكرة الأرضيّة
map	χarīṭa (f)	خريطة
atlas	aṭlas (m)	أطلس
Europe	urūbba (f)	أوروبّا
Asia	'āsiya (f)	آسيا
Africa	afrīqiya (f)	أفريقيا
Australia	usturāliya (f)	أستراليا
America	amrīka (f)	أمريكا
North America	amrīka aʃ ʃimāliyya (f)	أمريكا الشماليّة

South America	amrīka al ʒanūbiyya (f)	أمريكا الجنوبيّة
Antarctica	al quṭb al ʒanūbiy (m)	القطب الجنوبيّ
the Arctic	al quṭb aʃʃimāliy (m)	القطب الشماليّ

76. Cardinal directions

north	ʃimāl (m)	شمال
to the north	ilaʃʃimāl	إلى الشمال
in the north	fiʃʃimāl	في الشمال
northern (adj)	ʃimāliy	شماليَ

south	ʒanūb (m)	جنوب
to the south	ilal ʒanūb	إلى الجنوب
in the south	fil ʒanūb	في الجنوب
southern (adj)	ʒanūbiy	جنوبي

west	ɣarb (m)	غرب
to the west	ilal ɣarb	إلى الغرب
in the west	fil ɣarb	في الغرب
western (adj)	ɣarbiy	غربي

east	ʃarq (m)	شرق
to the east	ilaʃ ʃarq	إلى الشرق
in the east	fiʃ ʃarq	في الشرق
eastern (adj)	ʃarqiy	شرقيَ

77. Sea. Ocean

sea	baḥr (m)	بحر
ocean	muḥīṭ (m)	محيط
gulf (bay)	χalīʒ (m)	خليج
straits	maḍīq (m)	مضيق

land (solid ground)	barr (m)	برَ
continent (mainland)	qārra (f)	قارّة
island	ʒazīra (f)	جزيرة
peninsula	ʃibh ʒazīra (f)	شبه جزيرة
archipelago	maʒmūʿat ʒuzur (f)	مجموعة جزر

bay, cove	χalīʒ (m)	خليج
harbor	mīnā' (m)	ميناء
lagoon	buḥayra ʃāṭiʿa (f)	بحيرة شاطئة
cape	ra's (m)	رأس

atoll	ʒazīra marʒāniyya istiwā'iyya (f)	جزيرة مرجانيّة إستوائيّة
reef	ʃiʿāb (pl)	شعاب
coral	murʒān (m)	مرجان

coral reef	ʃiʻāb marʒāniyya (pl)	شعاب مرجانيّة
deep (adj)	ʻamīq	عميق
depth (deep water)	ʻumq (m)	عمق
abyss	mahwāt (f)	مهواة
trench (e.g., Mariana ~)	xandaq (m)	خندق
current (Ocean ~)	tayyār (m)	تيّار
to surround (bathe)	aḥāṭ	أحاط
shore	sāḥil (m)	ساحل
coast	sāḥil (m)	ساحل
flow (flood tide)	madd (m)	مدّ
ebb (ebb tide)	ʒazr (m)	جزر
shoal	miyāh ḍaḥla (f)	مياه ضحلة
bottom (~ of the sea)	qāʻ (m)	قاع
wave	mawʒa (f)	موجة
crest (~ of a wave)	qimmat mawʒa (f)	قمّة موجة
spume (sea foam)	zabad al baḥr (m)	زبد البحر
storm (sea storm)	ʻāṣifa (f)	عاصفة
hurricane	iʻṣār (m)	إعصار
tsunami	tsunāmi (m)	تسونامي
calm (dead ~)	hudūʼ (m)	هدوء
quiet, calm (adj)	hādiʼ	هادئ
pole	quṭb (m)	قطب
polar (adj)	quṭby	قطبيّ
latitude	ʻarḍ (m)	عرض
longitude	ṭūl (m)	طول
parallel	mutawāzi (m)	متواز
equator	xaṭṭ al istiwāʼ (m)	خط الإستواء
sky	samāʼ (f)	سماء
horizon	ufuq (m)	أفق
air	hawāʼ (m)	هواء
lighthouse	manāra (f)	منارة
to dive (vi)	ɣāṣ	غاص
to sink (ab. boat)	ɣariq	غرق
treasures	kunūz (pl)	كنوز

78. Seas' and Oceans' names

Atlantic Ocean	al muḥīṭ al aṭlasiy (m)	المحيط الأطلسيّ
Indian Ocean	al muḥīṭ al hindiy (m)	المحيط الهنديّ
Pacific Ocean	al muḥīṭ al hādiʼ (m)	المحيط الهادئ
Arctic Ocean	al muḥīṭ il mutaʒammid aʃʃimāliy (m)	المحيط المتجمّد الشماليّ

Black Sea	al baḥr al aswad (m)	البحر الأسود
Red Sea	al baḥr al aḥmar (m)	البحر الأحمر
Yellow Sea	al baḥr al aṣfar (m)	البحر الأصفر
White Sea	al baḥr al abyaḍ (m)	البحر الأبيض

Caspian Sea	baḥr qazwīn (m)	بحر قزوين
Dead Sea	al baḥr al mayyit (m)	البحر الميّت
Mediterranean Sea	al baḥr al abyaḍ al mutawassiṭ (m)	البحر الأبيض المتوسّط

| Aegean Sea | baḥr īʒah (m) | بحر إيجة |
| Adriatic Sea | al baḥr al adriyatīkiy (m) | البحر الأدرياتيكيّ |

Arabian Sea	baḥr al ʿarab (m)	بحر العرب
Sea of Japan	baḥr al yabān (m)	بحر اليابان
Bering Sea	baḥr birinʒ (m)	بحر بيرينغ
South China Sea	baḥr aṣ ṣīn al ʒanūbiy (m)	بحر الصين الجنوبيّ

Coral Sea	baḥr al marʒān (m)	بحر المرجان
Tasman Sea	baḥr tasmān (m)	بحر تسمان
Caribbean Sea	al baḥr al karībiy (m)	البحر الكاريبيّ

| Barents Sea | baḥr barints (m) | بحر بارينس |
| Kara Sea | baḥr kara (m) | بحر كارا |

North Sea	baḥr aʃ ʃimāl (m)	بحر الشمال
Baltic Sea	al baḥr al balṭīq (m)	البحر البلطيق
Norwegian Sea	baḥr an narwīʒ (m)	بحر النرويج

79. Mountains

mountain	ʒabal (m)	جبل
mountain range	silsilat ʒibāl (f)	سلسلة جبال
mountain ridge	qimam ʒabaliyya (pl)	قمم جبليّة

summit, top	qimma (f)	قمّة
peak	qimma (f)	قمّة
foot (~ of the mountain)	asfal (m)	أسفل
slope (mountainside)	munḥadar (m)	منحدر

volcano	burkān (m)	بركان
active volcano	burkān naʃiṭ (m)	بركان نشط
dormant volcano	burkān xāmid (m)	بركان خامد

eruption	θawrān (m)	ثوران
crater	fūhat al burkān (f)	فوهة البركان
magma	māɣma (f)	ماغما
lava	ḥumam burkāniyya (pl)	حمم بركانيّة
molten (~ lava)	munṣahira	منصهرة
canyon	talʿa (m)	تلعة

gorge	wādi dayyiq (m)	واد ضيّق
crevice	ʃaqq (m)	شقّ
abyss (chasm)	hāwiya (f)	هاوية

pass, col	mamarr ʒabaliy (m)	ممرّ جبليّ
plateau	hadba (f)	هضبة
cliff	ʒurf (m)	جرف
hill	tall (m)	تلّ

glacier	nahr ʒalīdiy (m)	نهر جليديّ
waterfall	ʃallāl (m)	شلال
geyser	fawwāra hārra (m)	فوّارة حارّة
lake	buhayra (f)	بحيرة

plain	sahl (m)	سهل
landscape	manzar tabīʿiy (m)	منظر طبيعيّ
echo	sada (m)	صدى

alpinist	mutasalliq al ʒibāl (m)	متسلّق الجبال
rock climber	mutasalliq suxūr (m)	متسلّق صخور
to conquer (in climbing)	tayallab ʿala	تغلّب على
climb (an easy ~)	tasalluq (m)	تسلّق

80. Mountains names

The Alps	ʒibāl al alb (pl)	جبال الألب
Mont Blanc	mūn blūn (m)	مون بلون
The Pyrenees	ʒibāl al barānis (pl)	جبال البرانس

The Carpathians	ʒibāl al karbāt (pl)	جبال الكاربات
The Ural Mountains	ʒibāl al ʿūrāl (pl)	جبال الأورال
The Caucasus Mountains	ʒibāl al qawqāz (pl)	جبال القوقاز
Mount Elbrus	ʒabal ilbrūs (m)	جبل إلبروس

The Altai Mountains	ʒibāl altāy (pl)	جبال ألتاي
The Tian Shan	ʒibāl tian ʃan (pl)	جبال تيان شان
The Pamir Mountains	ʒibāl bamīr (pl)	جبال بامير
The Himalayas	himalāya (pl)	هيمالايا
Mount Everest	ʒabal ivirist (m)	جبل افرست

The Andes	ʒibāl al andīz (pl)	جبال الأنديز
Mount Kilimanjaro	ʒabal kilimanʒāru (m)	جبل كليمنجارو

81. Rivers

river	nahr (m)	نهر
spring (natural source)	ʿayn (m)	عين
riverbed (river channel)	maʒra an nahr (m)	مجرى النهر

basin (river valley)	ḥawḍ (m)	حوض
to flow into ...	ṣabb fi ...	...صبّ في
tributary	rāfid (m)	رافد
bank (of river)	ḍiffa (f)	ضفّة
current (stream)	tayyār (m)	تيّار
downstream (adv)	f ittiʒāh maʒra an nahr	في إتجاه مجرى النهر
upstream (adv)	ḍidd at tayyār	ضدّ التيّار
inundation	ɣamr (m)	غمر
flooding	fayaḍān (m)	فيضان
to overflow (vi)	fāḍ	فاض
to flood (vt)	ɣamar	غمر
shallow (shoal)	miyāh ḍaḥla (f)	مياه ضحلة
rapids	munḥadar an nahr (m)	منحدر النهر
dam	sadd (m)	سدّ
canal	qanāt (f)	قناة
reservoir (artificial lake)	χazzān māʼiy (m)	خزّان مائيّ
sluice, lock	hawīs (m)	هويس
water body (pond, etc.)	masṭaḥ māʼiy (m)	مسطح مائيّ
swamp (marshland)	mustanqaʻ (m)	مستنقع
bog, marsh	mustanqaʻ (m)	مستنقع
whirlpool	dawwāma (f)	دوّامة
stream (brook)	ʒadwal māʼiy (m)	جدول مائيّ
drinking (ab. water)	aʃ ʃurb	الشرب
fresh (~ water)	ʻaðb	عذب
ice	ʒalīd (m)	جليد
to freeze over (ab. river, etc.)	taʒammad	تجمّد

82. Rivers' names

Seine	nahr as sīn (m)	نهر السين
Loire	nahr al lua:r (m)	نهر اللوار
Thames	nahr at tīmz (m)	نهر التيمز
Rhine	nahr ar rayn (m)	نهر الراين
Danube	nahr ad danūb (m)	نهر الدانوب
Volga	nahr al vulɣa (m)	نهر الفولغا
Don	nahr ad dūn (m)	نهر الدون
Lena	nahr līna (m)	نهر لينا
Yellow River	an nahr al aṣfar (m)	النهر الأصفر
Yangtze	nahr al yanɣtsi (m)	نهر اليانغتسي

| Mekong | nahr al mikunɣ (m) | نهر الميكونغ |
| Ganges | nahr al ɣānʒ (m) | نهر الغانج |

Nile River	nahr an nīl (m)	نهر النيل
Congo River	nahr al kunɣu (m)	نهر الكونغو
Okavango River	nahr ukavanʒu (m)	نهر اوكافانجو
Zambezi River	nahr az zambizi (m)	نهر الزمبيزي
Limpopo River	nahr limbubu (m)	نهر ليمبوبو
Mississippi River	nahr al mississibbi (m)	نهر الميسيسيبي

83. Forest

| forest, wood | ɣāba (f) | غابة |
| forest (as adj) | ɣāba | غابة |

thick forest	ɣāba kaθīfa (f)	غابة كثيفة
grove	ɣāba s̩aɣīra (f)	غابة صغيرة
forest clearing	minţaqa uzīlat minha al aʃʒār (f)	منطقة أزيلت منها الأشجار

| thicket | aʒama (f) | أجمة |
| scrubland | ʃuʒayrāt (pl) | شجيرات |

| footpath (troddenpath) | mamarr (m) | ممرّ |
| gully | wādi ḑayyiq (m) | واد ضيّق |

tree	ʃaʒara (f)	شجرة
leaf	waraqa (f)	ورقة
leaves (foliage)	waraq (m)	ورق

fall of leaves	tasāquţ al awrāq (m)	تساقط الأوراق
to fall (ab. leaves)	saqaţ	سقط
top (of the tree)	ra's (m)	رأس

branch	ɣus̩n (m)	غصن
bough	ɣus̩n (m)	غصن
bud (on shrub, tree)	bur'um (m)	برعم
needle (of pine tree)	ʃawka (f)	شوكة
pine cone	kūz as̩ s̩anawbar (m)	كوز الصنوبر

hollow (in a tree)	ʒawf (m)	جوف
nest	'uʃʃ (m)	عشّ
burrow (animal hole)	ʒuhr (m)	جحر

trunk	ʒiðʕ (m)	جذع
root	ʒiðr (m)	جذر
bark	liħā' (m)	لحاء
moss	ţuħlub (m)	طحلب
to uproot (remove trees or tree stumps)	iqtala'	إقتلع

to chop down	qaṭaʿ	قطع
to deforest (vt)	azāl al ɣābāt	أزال الغابات
tree stump	ȝiðʿ aʃ ʃaȝara (m)	جذع الشجرة
campfire	nār muxayyam (m)	نار مخيّم
forest fire	ḥarīq ɣāba (m)	حريق غابة
to extinguish (vt)	aṭfaʾ	أطفأ
forest ranger	ḥāris al ɣāba (m)	حارس الغابة
protection	ḥimāya (f)	حماية
to protect (~ nature)	ḥama	حمى
poacher	sāriq aṣ ṣayd (m)	سارق الصيد
steel trap	maṣyada (f)	مصيدة
to gather, to pick (vt)	ȝamaʿ	جمع
to lose one's way	tāh	تاه

84. Natural resources

natural resources	θarawāt ṭabīʿiyya (pl)	ثروات طبيعيّة
minerals	maʿādin (pl)	معادن
deposits	makāmin (pl)	مكامن
field (e.g., oilfield)	ḥaql (m)	حقل
to mine (extract)	istaxraȝ	إستخرج
mining (extraction)	istixrāȝ (m)	إستخراج
ore	xām (m)	خام
mine (e.g., for coal)	manȝam (m)	منجم
shaft (mine ~)	manȝam (m)	منجم
miner	ʿāmil manȝam (m)	عامل منجم
gas (natural ~)	ɣāz (m)	غاز
gas pipeline	xaṭṭ anābīb ɣāz (m)	خط أنابيب غاز
oil (petroleum)	nafṭ (m)	نفط
oil pipeline	anābīb an nafṭ (pl)	أنابيب النفط
oil well	biʾr an nafṭ (m)	بئر النفط
derrick (tower)	ḥaffāra (f)	حفّارة
tanker	nāqilat an nafṭ (f)	ناقلة النفط
sand	raml (m)	رمل
limestone	ḥaȝar kalsiy (m)	حجر كلسيّ
gravel	ḥaṣa (m)	حصى
peat	xaθθ faḥm nabātiy (m)	خثّ فحم نباتيّ
clay	ṭīn (m)	طين
coal	faḥm (m)	فحم
iron (ore)	ḥadīd (m)	حديد
gold	ðahab (m)	ذهب
silver	fiḍḍa (f)	فضّة

| nickel | nikil (m) | نيكل |
| copper | nuḥās (m) | نحاس |

zinc	zink (m)	زنك
manganese	manɣanīz (m)	منغنيز
mercury	zi'baq (m)	زئبق
lead	ruṣāṣ (m)	رصاص

mineral	maʿdan (m)	معدن
crystal	ballūra (f)	بلّورة
marble	ruxām (m)	رخام
uranium	yurānuim (m)	يورانيوم

85. Weather

weather	ṭaqs (m)	طقس
weather forecast	naʃra ʒawwiyya (f)	نشرة جوّية
temperature	ḥarāra (f)	حرارة
thermometer	tirmūmitr (m)	ترمومتر
barometer	barūmitr (m)	بارومتر

humid (adj)	raṭib	رطب
humidity	ruṭūba (f)	رطوبة
heat (extreme ~)	ḥarāra (f)	حرارة
hot (torrid)	ḥārr	حارّ
it's hot	al ʒaww ḥārr	الجوّ حارّ

| it's warm | al ʒaww dāfi' | الجوّ دافئ |
| warm (moderately hot) | dāfi' | دافئ |

| it's cold | al ʒaww bārid | الجوّ بارد |
| cold (adj) | bārid | بارد |

sun	ʃams (f)	شمس
to shine (vi)	aḍā'	أضاء
sunny (day)	muʃmis	مشمس
to come up (vi)	ʃaraq	شرق
to set (vi)	ɣarab	غرب

cloud	saḥāba (f)	سحابة
cloudy (adj)	ɣā'im	غائم
rain cloud	saḥābat maṭar (f)	سحابة مطر
somber (gloomy)	ɣā'im	غائم

rain	maṭar (m)	مطر
it's raining	innaha tamṭur	إنّها تمطر
rainy (~ day, weather)	mumṭir	ممطر
to drizzle (vi)	raðð	رذّ
pouring rain	maṭar munhamir (f)	مطر منهمر
downpour	maṭar ɣazīr (m)	مطر غزير

heavy (e.g., ~ rain)	ʃadīd	شديد
puddle	birka (f)	بركة
to get wet (in rain)	ibtall	إبتلّ

fog (mist)	ḍabāb (m)	ضباب
foggy	muḍabbab	مضبّب
snow	θalʒ (m)	ثلج
it's snowing	innaha taθluʒ	إنّها تثلج

86. Severe weather. Natural disasters

thunderstorm	ʻāṣifa raʻdiyya (f)	عاصفة رعديّة
lightning (~ strike)	barq (m)	برق
to flash (vi)	baraq	برق

thunder	raʻd (m)	رعد
to thunder (vi)	raʻad	رعد
it's thundering	tarʻad as samā'	ترعد السماء

| hail | maṭar bard (m) | مطر برد |
| it's hailing | tamṭur as samā' bardan | تمطر السماء بردًا |

| to flood (vt) | ɣamar | غمر |
| flood, inundation | fayaḍān (m) | فيضان |

earthquake	zilzāl (m)	زلزال
tremor, quake	hazza arḍiyya (f)	هزّة أرضيّة
epicenter	markaz az zilzāl (m)	مركز الزلزال

| eruption | θawrān (m) | ثوران |
| lava | ḥumam burkāniyya (pl) | حمم بركانيّة |

| twister, tornado | iʻṣār (m) | إعصار |
| typhoon | ṭūfān (m) | طوفان |

hurricane	iʻṣār (m)	إعصار
storm	ʻāṣifa (f)	عاصفة
tsunami	tsunāmi (m)	تسونامي

cyclone	iʻṣār (m)	إعصار
bad weather	ṭaqs sayyi' (m)	طقس سيّء
fire (accident)	ḥarīq (m)	حريق

| disaster | kāriθa (f) | كارثة |
| meteorite | ḥaʒar nayzakiy (m) | حجر نيزكيّ |

avalanche	inhiyār θalʒiy (m)	إنهيار ثلجيّ
snowslide	inhiyār θalʒiy (m)	إنهيار ثلجيّ
blizzard	ʻāṣifa θalʒiyya (f)	عاصفة ثلجيّة
snowstorm	ʻāṣifa θalʒiyya (f)	عاصفة ثلجيّة

FAUNA

87. Mammals. Predators
88. Wild animals
89. Domestic animals
90. Birds
91. Fish. Marine animals
92. Amphibians. Reptiles
93. Insects

T&P Books Publishing

87. Mammals. Predators

predator	ḥayawān muftaris (m)	حيوان مفترس
tiger	namir (m)	نمر
lion	asad (m)	أسد
wolf	ði'b (m)	ذئب
fox	θaʿlab (m)	ثعلب
jaguar	namir amrīkiy (m)	نمر أمريكيّ
leopard	fahd (m)	فهد
cheetah	namir ṣayyād (m)	نمر صيّاد
black panther	namir aswad (m)	نمر أسود
puma	būma (m)	بوما
snow leopard	namir aθ θulūʒ (m)	نمر الثلوج
lynx	waʃaq (m)	وشق
coyote	qayūṭ (m)	قيوط
jackal	ibn 'āwa (m)	ابن آوى
hyena	ḍabuʿ (m)	ضبع

88. Wild animals

animal	ḥayawān (m)	حيوان
beast (animal)	ḥayawān (m)	حيوان
squirrel	sinʒāb (m)	سنجاب
hedgehog	qumfuð (m)	قنفذ
hare	arnab barriy (m)	أرنب برّيّ
rabbit	arnab (m)	أرنب
badger	ɣarīr (m)	غرير
raccoon	rākūn (m)	راكون
hamster	qidād (m)	قداد
marmot	marmuṭ (m)	مرموط
mole	χuld (m)	خلد
mouse	fa'r (m)	فأر
rat	ʒurað (m)	جرذ
bat	χuffāʃ (m)	خفّاش
ermine	qāqum (m)	قاقم
sable	sammūr (m)	سمّور
marten	dalaq (m)	دلق

| weasel | ibn 'irs (m) | إبن عرس |
| mink | mink (m) | منك |

| beaver | qundus (m) | قندس |
| otter | quḍā'a (f) | قضاعة |

horse	ḥiṣān (m)	حصان
moose	mūz (m)	موظ
deer	ayyil (m)	أيّل
camel	ʒamal (m)	جمل

bison	bisūn (m)	بيسون
aurochs	θawr barriy (m)	ثور برّيّ
buffalo	ʒāmūs (m)	جاموس

zebra	ḥimār zarad (m)	حمار زرد
antelope	ẓabiy (m)	ظبي
roe deer	yaḥmūr (m)	يحمور
fallow deer	ayyil asmar urubbiy (m)	أيّل أسمر أوروبيّ
chamois	ʃamwāh (f)	شاموه
wild boar	xinzīr barriy (m)	خنزير برّيّ

whale	ḥūt (m)	حوت
seal	fuqma (f)	فقمة
walrus	faẓẓ (m)	فظّ
fur seal	fuqmat al firā' (f)	فقمة الفراء
dolphin	dilfīn (m)	دلفين

bear	dubb (m)	دبّ
polar bear	dubb quṭbiy (m)	دبّ قطبيّ
panda	bānda (m)	باندا

monkey	qird (m)	قرد
chimpanzee	ʃimbanzi (m)	شيمبانزي
orangutan	urangutān (m)	أورنغوتان
gorilla	ɣurīlla (f)	غوريلا
macaque	qird al makāk (m)	قرد المكاك
gibbon	ʒibbūn (m)	جيبون

| elephant | fīl (m) | فيل |
| rhinoceros | xartīt (m) | خرتيت |

| giraffe | zarāfa (f) | زرافة |
| hippopotamus | faras an nahr (m) | فرس النهر |

| kangaroo | kanɣar (m) | كنغر |
| koala (bear) | kuala (m) | كوالا |

mongoose	nims (m)	نمس
chinchilla	ʃinʃila (f)	شنشيلة
skunk	ẓaribān (m)	ظربان
porcupine	nīṣ (m)	نيص

89. Domestic animals

cat	qiṭṭa (f)	قطة
tomcat	ðakar al qiṭṭ (m)	ذكر القطّ
dog	kalb (m)	كلب
horse	ḥiṣān (m)	حصان
stallion (male horse)	faḥl al xayl (m)	فحل الخيل
mare	unθa al faras (f)	أنثى الفرس
cow	baqara (f)	بقرة
bull	θawr (m)	ثور
ox	θawr (m)	ثور
sheep (ewe)	xarūf (f)	خروف
ram	kabʃ (m)	كبش
goat	mā'iz (m)	ماعز
billy goat, he-goat	ðakar al mā'ið (m)	ذكر الماعز
donkey	ḥimār (m)	حمار
mule	bayl (m)	بغل
pig, hog	xinzīr (m)	خنزير
piglet	xannūṣ (m)	خنّوص
rabbit	arnab (m)	أرنب
hen (chicken)	daʒāʒa (f)	دجاجة
rooster	dīk (m)	ديك
duck	baṭṭa (f)	بطة
drake	ðakar al baṭṭ (m)	ذكر البطّ
goose	iwazza (f)	إوزّة
tom turkey, gobbler	dīk rūmiy (m)	ديك رومي
turkey (hen)	daʒāʒ rūmiy (m)	دجاج رومي
domestic animals	ḥayawānāt dawāʒin (pl)	حيوانات دواجن
tame (e.g., ~ hamster)	alīf	أليف
to tame (vt)	allaf	ألّف
to breed (vt)	rabba	ربّى
farm	mazra'a (f)	مزرعة
poultry	ṭuyūr dāʒina (pl)	طيور داجنة
cattle	māʃiya (f)	ماشية
herd (cattle)	qaṭī' (m)	قطيع
stable	isṭabl xayl (m)	إسطبل خيل
pigpen	ḥaẓīrat al xanāzīr (f)	حظيرة الخنازير
cowshed	zirībat al baqar (f)	زريبة البقر
rabbit hutch	qunn al arānib (m)	قنّ الأرانب
hen house	qunn ad daʒāʒ (m)	قن الدجاج

90. Birds

bird	ṭā'ir (m)	طائر
pigeon	ḥamāma (f)	حمامة
sparrow	'uṣfūr (m)	عصفور
tit (great tit)	qurquf (m)	قرقف
magpie	'aq'aq (m)	عقعق
raven	ɣurāb aswad (m)	غراب أسود
crow	ɣurāb (m)	غراب
jackdaw	zāɣ (m)	زاغ
rook	ɣurāb al qayẓ (m)	غراب القيظ
duck	baṭṭa (f)	بطة
goose	iwazza (f)	إوزة
pheasant	tadarruʒ (m)	تدرج
eagle	nasr (m)	نسر
hawk	bāz (m)	باز
falcon	ṣaqr (m)	صقر
vulture	raχam (m)	رخم
condor (Andean ~)	kundūr (m)	كندور
swan	timma (m)	تمة
crane	kurkiy (m)	كركي
stork	laqlaq (m)	لقلق
parrot	babaɣā' (m)	ببغاء
hummingbird	ṭannān (m)	طنّان
peacock	ṭāwūs (m)	طاووس
ostrich	na'āma (f)	نعامة
heron	balaʃūn (m)	بلشون
flamingo	nuḥām wardiy (m)	نحام وردي
pelican	baʒa'a (f)	بجعة
nightingale	bulbul (m)	بلبل
swallow	sunūnū (m)	سنونو
thrush	sumna (m)	سمنة
song thrush	summuna muɣarrida (m)	سمنة مغرّدة
blackbird	ʃaḥrūr aswad (m)	شحرور أسود
swift	samāma (m)	سمامة
lark	qubbara (f)	قبّرة
quail	sammān (m)	سمّان
woodpecker	naqqār al χaʃab (m)	نقّار الخشب
cuckoo	waqwāq (m)	وقواق
owl	būma (f)	بومة
eagle owl	būm urāsiy (m)	بوم أوراسيّ

wood grouse	dīk il χalanʒ (m)	ديك الخلنج
black grouse	ṭayhūʒ aswad (m)	طيهوج أسود
partridge	haʒal (m)	حجل

starling	zurzūr (m)	زرزور
canary	kanāriy (m)	كناريّ
hazel grouse	ṭayhūʒ il bunduq (m)	طيهوج البندق
chaffinch	ʃurʃūr (m)	شرشور
bullfinch	diχnāʃ (m)	دغناش

seagull	nawras (m)	نورس
albatross	al qaṭras (m)	القطرس
penguin	biṭrīq (m)	بطريق

91. Fish. Marine animals

bream	abramīs (m)	أبراميس
carp	ʃabbūṭ (m)	شبّوط
perch	farχ (m)	فرخ
catfish	qarmūṭ (m)	قرموط
pike	samak al karāki (m)	سمك الكراكي

| salmon | salmūn (m) | سلمون |
| sturgeon | haʃʃ (m) | حفش |

herring	rinʒa (f)	رنجة
Atlantic salmon	salmūn aṭlasiy (m)	سلمون أطلسيّ
mackerel	usqumriy (m)	أسقمريّ
flatfish	samak mufalṭah (f)	سمك مفلطح

zander, pike perch	samak sandar (m)	سمك سندر
cod	qudd (m)	قدّ
tuna	tūna (f)	تونة
trout	salmūn muraqqaṭ (m)	سلمون مرقّط

eel	hankalīs (m)	حنكليس
electric ray	ra''ād (m)	رعّاد
moray eel	murāy (m)	موراي
piranha	birāna (f)	بيرانا

shark	qirʃ (m)	قرش
dolphin	dilfīn (m)	دلفين
whale	hūt (m)	حوت

crab	salṭaʿūn (m)	سلطعون
jellyfish	qindīl al bahr (m)	قنديل البحر
octopus	uχṭubūṭ (m)	أخطبوط

| starfish | naʒmat al bahr (f) | نجمة البحر |
| sea urchin | qumfuð al bahr (m) | قنفذ البحر |

seahorse	ḥiṣān al baḥr (m)	فرس البحر
oyster	maḥār (m)	محار
shrimp	ʒambari (m)	جمبري
lobster	istakūza (f)	إستكوزا
spiny lobster	karkand ʃāik (m)	كركند شائك

92. Amphibians. Reptiles

| snake | θuʕbān (m) | ثعبان |
| venomous (snake) | sāmm | سامّ |

viper	afʕa (f)	أفعى
cobra	kūbra (m)	كوبرا
python	biθūn (m)	بيثون
boa	buwāʼ (f)	بواء

grass snake	θuʕbān al ʕuʃb (m)	ثعبان العشب
rattle snake	afʕa al ʒalʒala (f)	أفعى الجلجلة
anaconda	anakūnda (f)	أناكوندا

lizard	siḥliyya (f)	سحليّة
iguana	iɣwāna (f)	إغوانة
monitor lizard	waral (m)	ورل
salamander	samandar (m)	سمندر
chameleon	ḥirbāʼ (f)	حرباء
scorpion	ʕaqrab (m)	عقرب

turtle	sulaḥfāt (f)	سلحفاة
frog	ḍifdaʕ (m)	ضفدع
toad	ḍifdaʕ aṭ ṭīn (m)	ضفدع الطين
crocodile	timsāḥ (m)	تمساح

93. Insects

insect, bug	ḥaʃara (f)	حشرة
butterfly	farāʃa (f)	فراشة
ant	namla (f)	نملة
fly	ðubāba (f)	ذبابة
mosquito	namūsa (f)	ناموسة
beetle	χunfusa (f)	خنفسة

wasp	dabbūr (m)	دبّور
bee	naḥla (f)	نحلة
bumblebee	naḥla ṭannāna (f)	نحلة طنّانة
gadfly (botfly)	naʕra (f)	نعرة

| spider | ʕankabūt (m) | عنكبوت |
| spiderweb | nasīʒ ʕankabūt (m) | نسيج عنكبوت |

dragonfly	ya'sūb (m)	يعسوب
grasshopper	ʒarād (m)	جراد
moth (night butterfly)	'itta (f)	عتّة
cockroach	ṣurṣūr (m)	صرصور
tick	qurāda (f)	قرادة
flea	burɣūθ (m)	برغوث
midge	ba'ūḍa (f)	بعوضة
locust	ʒarād (m)	جراد
snail	ḥalzūn (m)	حلزون
cricket	ṣarrār al layl (m)	صرّار الليل
lightning bug	yarā'a muḍī'a (f)	يراعة مضيئة
ladybug	da'sūqa (f)	دعسوقة
cockchafer	χunfusa kabīra (f)	خنفسة كبيرة
leech	'alaqa (f)	علقة
caterpillar	yasrū' (m)	يسروع
earthworm	dūda (f)	دودة
larva	yaraqa (f)	يرقة

T&P BOOKS

FLORA

94. Trees
95. Shrubs
96. Fruits. Berries
97. Flowers. Plants
98. Cereals, grains

T&P Books Publishing

tree	ʃaʒara (f)	شجرة
deciduous (adj)	nafḍiyya	نفضيّة
coniferous (adj)	ṣanawbariyya	صنوبريّة
evergreen (adj)	dā'imat al ҳuḍra	دائمة الخضرة
apple tree	ʃaʒarat tuffāḥ (f)	شجرة تفّاح
pear tree	ʃaʒarat kummaθra (f)	شجرة كمّثرى
cherry tree	ʃaʒarat karaz (f)	شجرة كرز
plum tree	ʃaʒarat barqūq (f)	شجرة برقوق
birch	batūla (f)	بتولا
oak	ballūṭ (f)	بلّوط
linden tree	ʃaʒarat zayzafūn (f)	شجرة زيزفون
aspen	ḥawr raʒrāʒ (m)	حور رجراج
maple	qayqab (f)	قيقب
spruce	ratinaʒ (f)	راتينج
pine	ṣanawbar (f)	صنوبر
larch	arziyya (f)	أرزيّة
fir tree	tannūb (f)	تنّوب
cedar	arz (f)	أرز
poplar	ḥawr (f)	حور
rowan	ɣubayrā' (f)	غبيراء
willow	ṣafṣāf (f)	صفصاف
alder	ʒār il mā' (m)	جار الماء
beech	zān (m)	زان
elm	dardār (f)	دردار
ash (tree)	marān (f)	مران
chestnut	kastanā' (f)	كستناء
magnolia	maɣnūliya (f)	مغنوليا
palm tree	naҳla (f)	نخلة
cypress	sarw (f)	سرو
mangrove	ayka sāḥiliyya (f)	أيكة ساحليّة
baobab	bāubāb (f)	باوباب
eucalyptus	ukaliptus (f)	أوكاليبتوس
sequoia	siqūya (f)	سيكويا

95. Shrubs

bush	ʃuʒayra (f)	شجيرة
shrub	ʃuʒayrāt (pl)	شجيرات
grapevine	karma (f)	كرمة
vineyard	karam (m)	كرم
raspberry bush	tūt al ʻullayq al aḥmar (m)	توت العلّيق الأحمر
redcurrant bush	kiʃmiʃ aḥmar (m)	كشمش أحمر
gooseberry bush	ʻinab aθ θaʻlab (m)	عنب الثعلب
acacia	sanṭ (f)	سنط
barberry	amīr barīs (m)	أمير باريس
jasmine	yāsmīn (m)	ياسمين
juniper	ʻarʻar (m)	عرعر
rosebush	ʃuʒayrat ward (f)	شجيرة ورد
dog rose	ward ʒabaliy (m)	ورد جبليّ

96. Fruits. Berries

fruit	θamra (f)	ثمرة
fruits	θamr (m)	ثمر
apple	tuffāḥa (f)	تفّاحة
pear	kummaθra (f)	كمثرى
plum	barqūq (m)	برقوق
strawberry (garden ~)	farawla (f)	فراولة
cherry	karaz (m)	كرز
grape	ʻinab (m)	عنب
raspberry	tūt al ʻullayq al aḥmar (m)	توت العلّيق الأحمر
blackcurrant	ʻinab aθ θaʻlab al aswad (m)	عنب الثعلب الأسود
redcurrant	kiʃmiʃ aḥmar (m)	كشمش أحمر
gooseberry	ʻinab aθ θaʻlab (m)	عنب الثعلب
cranberry	tūt aḥmar barriy (m)	توت أحمر برّيَ
orange	burtuqāl (m)	برتقال
mandarin	yūsufiy (m)	يوسفي
pineapple	ananās (m)	أناناس
banana	mawz (m)	موز
date	tamr (m)	تمر
lemon	laymūn (m)	ليمون
apricot	miʃmiʃ (f)	مشمش
peach	durrāq (m)	دراق
kiwi	kiwi (m)	كيوي

grapefruit	zinbāʿ (m)	زنباع
berry	ḥabba (f)	حبّة
berries	ḥabbāt (pl)	حبّات
cowberry	ʿinab aθ θawr (m)	عنب الثور
wild strawberry	farāwla barriyya (f)	فراولة برّية
bilberry	ʿinab al aḥrāʒ (m)	عنب الأحراج

97. Flowers. Plants

| flower | zahra (f) | زهرة |
| bouquet (of flowers) | bāqat zuhūr (f) | باقة زهور |

rose (flower)	warda (f)	وردة
tulip	tulīb (f)	توليب
carnation	qurumful (m)	قرنفل
gladiolus	dalbūθ (f)	دلبوث

cornflower	turunʃāh (m)	ترنشاه
harebell	ʒarīs (m)	جريس
dandelion	hindibāʾ (f)	هندباء
camomile	babunʒ (m)	بابونج

aloe	aluwwa (m)	ألوّة
cactus	ṣabbār (m)	صبّار
rubber plant, ficus	tīn (m)	تين

lily	sawsan (m)	سوسن
geranium	ibrat ar rāʿi (f)	إبرة الراعي
hyacinth	zanbaq (f)	زنبق

mimosa	mimūza (f)	ميموزا
narcissus	narʒis (f)	نرجس
nasturtium	abu xanʒar (f)	أبو خنجر

orchid	saḥlab (f)	سحلب
peony	fawniya (f)	فاوانيا
violet	banafsaʒ (f)	بنفسج

pansy	banafsaʒ muθallaθ (m)	بنفسج مثلّث
forget-me-not	ʾāðān al faʾr (pl)	آذان الفأر
daisy	uqḥuwān (f)	أقحوان

poppy	xaʃxāʃ (f)	خشخاش
hemp	qinnab (m)	قنب
mint	naʿnāʿ (m)	نعناع

lily of the valley	sawsan al wādi (m)	سوسن الوادي
snowdrop	zahrat al laban (f)	زهرة اللبن
nettle	qarrāṣ (m)	قرّاص
sorrel	ḥammāḍ (m)	حمّاض

water lily	nilūfar (m)	نيلوفر
fern	saraxs (m)	سرخس
lichen	uʃna (f)	أشنة

greenhouse (tropical ~)	daffʼa (f)	دفيئة
lawn	ʻuʃb (m)	عشب
flowerbed	ʒunaynat zuhūr (f)	جنينة زهور

plant	nabāt (m)	نبات
grass	ʻuʃb (m)	عشب
blade of grass	ʻuʃba (f)	عشبة

leaf	waraqa (f)	ورقة
petal	waraqat az zahra (f)	ورقة الزهرة
stem	sāq (f)	ساق
tuber	darnat nabāt (f)	درنة نبات

| young plant (shoot) | nabta sayīra (f) | نبتة صغيرة |
| thorn | ʃawka (f) | شوكة |

to blossom (vi)	nawwar	نوّر
to fade, to wither	ðabal	ذبل
smell (odor)	rā'iḥa (f)	رائحة
to cut (flowers)	qataʻ	قطع
to pick (a flower)	qataf	قطف

98. Cereals, grains

grain	ḥubūb (pl)	حبوب
cereal crops	maḥāṣīl al ḥubūb (pl)	محاصيل الحبوب
ear (of barley, etc.)	sumbula (f)	سنبلة

wheat	qamḥ (m)	قمح
rye	ʒāwdār (m)	جاودار
oats	ʃūfān (m)	شوفان
millet	duxn (m)	دخن
barley	ʃaʼīr (m)	شعير

corn	ðura (f)	ذرّة
rice	urz (m)	أرز
buckwheat	ḥinta sawdā' (f)	حنطة سوداء

pea plant	bisilla (f)	بسلة
kidney bean	faṣūliya (f)	فاصوليا
soy	fūl aṣ ṣūya (m)	فول الصويا
lentil	ʻadas (m)	عدس
beans (pulse crops)	fūl (m)	فول

COUNTRIES OF
THE WORLD

99. Countries. Part 1
100. Countries. Part 2
101. Countries. Part 3

T&P Books Publishing

Afghanistan	afɣanistān (f)	أفغانستان
Albania	albāniya (f)	ألبانيا
Argentina	arʒantīn (f)	الأرجنتين
Armenia	armīniya (f)	أرمينيا
Australia	usturāliya (f)	أستراليا
Austria	an nimsa (f)	النمسا
Azerbaijan	aðarbiʒān (m)	أذربيجان
The Bahamas	ʒuzur bahāmas (pl)	جزر باهاماس
Bangladesh	banʒladīʃ (f)	بنجلاديش
Belarus	bilarūs (f)	بيلاروس
Belgium	balʒīka (f)	بلجيكا
Bolivia	bulīviya (f)	بوليفيا
Bosnia and Herzegovina	al busna wal hirsuk (f)	البوسنة والهرسك
Brazil	al brazīl (f)	البرازيل
Bulgaria	bulɣāriya (f)	بلغاريا
Cambodia	kambūdya (f)	كمبوديا
Canada	kanada (f)	كندا
Chile	tʃīli (f)	تشيلي
China	aṣ ṣīn (f)	الصين
Colombia	kulumbiya (f)	كولومبيا
Croatia	kruātiya (f)	كرواتيا
Cuba	kūba (f)	كوبا
Cyprus	qubruṣ (f)	قبرص
Czech Republic	atʃ tʃīk (f)	التشيك
Denmark	ad danimārk (f)	الدانمارك
Dominican Republic	ʒumhūriyyat ad duminikan (f)	جمهوريّة الدومينيكان
Ecuador	al iqwadūr (f)	الإكوادور
Egypt	miṣr (f)	مصر
England	inʒiltirra (f)	إنجلترًا
Estonia	istūniya (f)	إستونيا
Finland	finlanda (f)	فنلندا
France	faransa (f)	فرنسا
French Polynesia	bulinīziya al faransiyya (f)	بولينزيا الفرنسيّة
Georgia	ʒūrʒiya (f)	جورجيا
Germany	almāniya (f)	ألمانيا
Ghana	ɣāna (f)	غانا
Great Britain	briṭāniya al ʿuẓma (f)	بريطانيا العظمى
Greece	al yūnān (f)	اليونان
Haiti	haīti (f)	هايتي
Hungary	al maʒar (f)	المجر

100. Countries. Part 2

Iceland	'āyslanda (f)	آيسلندا
India	al hind (f)	الهند
Indonesia	indunīsiya (f)	إندونيسيا
Iran	ᵢīrān (f)	إيران
Iraq	al 'irāq (m)	العراق
Ireland	irlanda (f)	أيرلندا
Israel	isrā'īl (f)	إسرائيل
Italy	iṭāliya (f)	إيطاليا
Jamaica	ʒamāyka (f)	جامايكا
Japan	al yabān (f)	اليابان
Jordan	al urdun (m)	الأردن
Kazakhstan	kazaxstān (f)	كازاخستان
Kenya	kiniya (f)	كينيا
Kirghizia	qirɣizistān (f)	قيرغيزستان
Kuwait	al kuwayt (f)	الكويت
Laos	lawus (f)	لاوس
Latvia	lātviya (f)	لاتفيا
Lebanon	lubnān (f)	لبنان
Libya	lībiya (f)	ليبيا
Liechtenstein	liʃtinʃtāyn (m)	ليشتنشتاين
Lithuania	litwāniya (f)	ليتوانيا
Luxembourg	luksimburɣ (f)	لوكسمبورغ
Macedonia (Republic of ~)	maqdūniya (f)	مقدونيا
Madagascar	madaɣaʃqar (f)	مدغشقر
Malaysia	malīziya (f)	ماليزيا
Malta	malṭa (f)	مالطا
Mexico	al maksīk (f)	المكسيك
Moldova, Moldavia	muldāviya (f)	مولدافيا
Monaco	munāku (f)	موناكو
Mongolia	manɣūliya (f)	منغوليا
Montenegro	al ʒabal al aswad (m)	الجبل الأسود
Morocco	al maɣrib (m)	المغرب
Myanmar	myanmār (f)	ميانمار
Namibia	namībiya (f)	ناميبيا
Nepal	nibāl (f)	نيبال
Netherlands	hulanda (f)	هولندا
New Zealand	nyu zilanda (f)	نيوزيلندا
North Korea	kūria aʃ ʃimāliyya (f)	كوريا الشماليّة
Norway	an nirwīʒ (f)	النرويج

101. Countries. Part 3

| Pakistan | bakistān (f) | باكستان |
| Palestine | filisṭīn (f) | فلسطين |

Panama	banama (f)	بنما
Paraguay	baraɣwāy (f)	باراغواي
Peru	biru (f)	بيرو
Poland	bulanda (f)	بولندا
Portugal	al burtuɣāl (f)	البرتغال
Romania	rumāniya (f)	رومانيا
Russia	rūsiya (f)	روسيا
Saudi Arabia	as saʿūdiyya (f)	السعوديّة
Scotland	iskutlanda (f)	اسكتلندا
Senegal	as siniɣāl (f)	السنغال
Serbia	ṣirbiya (f)	صربيا
Slovakia	sluvākiya (f)	سلوفاكيا
Slovenia	sluvīniya (f)	سلوفينيا
South Africa	ʒumhūriyyat afrīqiya al ʒanūbiyya (f)	جمهريّة أفريقيا الجنويّة
South Korea	kuriya al ʒanūbiyya (f)	كوريا الجنويّة
Spain	isbāniya (f)	إسبانيا
Suriname	surinām (f)	سورينام
Sweden	as suwayd (f)	السويد
Switzerland	swīsra (f)	سويسرا
Syria	sūriya (f)	سوريا
Taiwan	taywān (f)	تايوان
Tajikistan	ṭaʒīkistān (f)	طاجيكستان
Tanzania	tanzāniya (f)	تنزانيا
Tasmania	tasmāniya (f)	تاسمانيا
Thailand	taylānd (f)	تايلاند
Tunisia	tūnis (f)	تونس
Turkey	turkiya (f)	تركيا
Turkmenistan	turkmānistān (f)	تركمانستان
Ukraine	ukrāniya (f)	أوكرانيا
United Arab Emirates	al imārāt al ʿarabiyya al muttaḥida (pl)	الإمارات العربيّة المتّحدة
United States of America	al wilāyāt al muttaḥida al amrīkiyya (pl)	الولايات المتّحدة الأمريكيّة
Uruguay	uruɣwāy (f)	الأوروغواي
Uzbekistan	uzbikistān (f)	أوزبكستان
Vatican	al vatikān (m)	الفاتيكان
Venezuela	vinizwiyla (f)	فنزويلا
Vietnam	vitnām (f)	فيتنام
Zanzibar	zanʒibār (f)	زنجبار

GASTRONOMIC GLOSSARY

This section contains a lot of words and terms associated with food. This dictionary will make it easier for you to understand the menu at a restaurant and choose the right dish

T&P Books Publishing

English-Arabic gastronomic glossary

aftertaste	al maðāq al 'āliq fil fam (m)	المذاق العالق فى الفم
almond	lawz (m)	لوز
anise	yānsūn (m)	يانسون
aperitif	ʃarāb (m)	شراب
appetite	ʃahiyya (f)	شهيّة
appetizer	muqabbilāt (pl)	مقبّلات
apple	tuffāḥa (f)	تفّاحة
apricot	miʃmiʃ (f)	مشمش
artichoke	xurʃūf (m)	خرشوف
asparagus	halyūn (m)	هليون
Atlantic salmon	salmūn aṭlasiy (m)	سلمون أطلسيّ
avocado	avukādu (f)	افوكاتو
bacon	bikūn (m)	بيكون
banana	mawz (m)	موز
barley	ʃa'īr (m)	شعير
bartender	bārman (m)	بارمان
basil	rīḥān (m)	ريحان
bay leaf	awrāq al ɣār (pl)	أوراق الغار
beans	fūl (m)	فول
beef	laḥm al baqar (m)	لحم البقر
beer	bīra (f)	بيرة
beetroot	banʒar (m)	بنجر
bell pepper	filfil (m)	فلفل
berries	ḥabbāt (pl)	حبّات
berry	ḥabba (f)	حبّة
bilberry	'inab al aḥrāʒ (m)	عنب الأحراج
birch bolete	fuṭr bulīṭ (m)	فطر بوليط
bitter	murr	مرّ
black coffee	qahwa sāda (f)	قهوة سادة
black pepper	filfil aswad (m)	فلفل أسود
black tea	ʃāy aswad (m)	شاي أسود
blackberry	θamar al 'ullayk (m)	ثمر العليّق
blackcurrant	'inab aθ θa'lab al aswad (m)	عنب الثعلب الأسود
boiled	maslūq	مسلوق
bottle opener	fattāḥa (f)	فتّاحة
bread	xubz (m)	خبز
breakfast	fuṭūr (m)	فطور
bream	abramīs (m)	أبراميس
broccoli	brukuli (m)	بركولي
Brussels sprouts	kurumb brūksil (m)	كرنب بروكسل
buckwheat	ḥinṭa sawdā' (f)	حنطة سوداء
butter	zubda (f)	زبدة
buttercream	krīmat zubda (f)	كريمة زبدة

cabbage	kurumb (m)	كرنب
cake	ka'k (m)	كعك
cake	tūrta (f)	تورتة
calorie	su'ra ḥarāriyya (f)	سعرة حراريّة
can opener	fattāḥa (f)	فتّاحة
candy	bumbūn (m)	بونبون
canned food	mu'allabāt (pl)	معلّبات
cappuccino	kaputʃīnu (m)	كابتشينو
caraway	karāwiya (f)	كراوية
carbohydrates	naʃawiyyāt (pl)	نشويّات
carbonated	mukarban	مكربن
carp	ʃabbūṭ (m)	شبّوط
carrot	ʒazar (m)	جزر
catfish	qarmūṭ (m)	قرموط
cauliflower	qarnabīṭ (m)	قرنبيط
caviar	kaviyār (m)	كافيار
celery	karafs (m)	كرفس
cep	fuṭr bulīṭ ma'kūl (m)	فطر بوليط مأكول
cereal crops	maḥāṣīl al ḥubūb (pl)	محاصيل الحبوب
cereal grains	ḥubūb (pl)	حبوب
champagne	ʃambāniya (f)	شمبانيا
chanterelle	fuṭr kwīzi (m)	فطر كويزي
check	ḥisāb (m)	حساب
cheese	ʒubna (f)	جبنة
chewing gum	'ilk (m)	علك
chicken	daʒāʒ (m)	دجاج
chocolate	ʃukulāta (f)	شكولاتة
chocolate	biʃ ʃukulāṭa	بالشكولاتة
cinnamon	qirfa (f)	قرفة
clear soup	maraq (m)	مرق
cloves	qurumful (m)	قرنفل
cocktail	kuktayl (m)	كوكتيل
coconut	ʒawz al hind (m)	جوز هند
cod	samak al qudd (m)	سمك القدّ
coffee	qahwa (f)	قهوة
coffee with milk	qahwa bil ḥalīb (f)	قهوة بالحليب
cognac	kunyāk (m)	كونياك
cold	bārid	بارد
condensed milk	ḥalīb mukaθθaf (m)	حليب مكثّف
condiment	tābil (m)	تابل
confectionery	ḥalawiyyāt (pl)	حلويّات
cookies	baskawīt (m)	بسكويت
coriander	kuzbara (f)	كزبرة
corkscrew	barrīma (f)	بّريمة
corn	ðura (f)	ذّرة
corn	ðura (f)	ذّرة
cornflakes	kurn fliks (m)	كورن فليكس
course, dish	waʒba (f)	وجبة
cowberry	'inab aθ θawr (m)	عنب الثور
crab	salṭa'ūn (m)	سلطعون
cranberry	tūt aḥmar barriy (m)	توت أحمر بّريّ
cream	krīma (f)	كريمة

crumb	futāta (f)	فتاتة
cucumber	χiyār (m)	خيار
cuisine	maṭbaχ (m)	مطبخ
cup	finʒān (m)	فنجان
dark beer	bīra γāmiqa (f)	بيرة غامقة
date	tamr (m)	تمر
death cap	fuṭr amānīt falusyāniy as sāmm (m)	فطر أمانيت فالوسياني السامّ
dessert	ḥalawiyyāt (pl)	حلويّات
diet	ḥimya γaðā'iyya (f)	حمية غذائية
dill	ʃabat (m)	شبت
dinner	'aʃā' (m)	عشاء
dried	muʒaffaf	مجفف
drinking water	mā' ʃurb (m)	ماء شرب
duck	baṭṭa (f)	بطّة
ear	sumbula (f)	سنبلة
edible mushroom	fuṭr ṣāliḥ lil akl (m)	فطر صالح للأكل
eel	ḥankalīs (m)	حنكليس
egg	bayḍa (f)	بيضة
egg white	bayāḍ al bayḍ (m)	بياض البيض
egg yolk	ṣafār al bayḍ (m)	صفار البيض
eggplant	bātinʒān (m)	باذنجان
eggs	bayḍ (m)	بيض
Enjoy your meal!	hanī'an marī'an!	هنيئًا مريئًا!
fats	duhūn (pl)	دهون
fig	tīn (m)	تين
filling	ḥaʃwa (f)	حشوة
fish	samak (m)	سمك
flatfish	samak mufalṭaḥ (f)	سمك مفلطح
flour	daqīq (m)	دقيق
fly agaric	fuṭr amānīt aṭ ṭā'ir as sāmm (m)	فطر أمانيت الطائر السامّ
food	akl (m)	أكل
fork	ʃawka (f)	شوكة
freshly squeezed juice	'aṣīr ṭāziʒ (m)	عصير طازج
fried	maqliy	مقليّ
fried eggs	bayḍ maqliy (m)	بيض مقليّ
frozen	muʒammad	مجمّد
fruit	fākiha (f)	فاكهة
fruits	θamr (m)	ثمر
game	ṣayd (m)	صيد
gammon	faχð χinzīr (m)	فخذ خنزير
garlic	θūm (m)	ثوم
gin	ʒīn (m)	جين
ginger	zanʒabīl (m)	زنجبيل
glass	kubbāya (f)	كبّاية
glass	ka's (f)	كأس
goose	iwazza (f)	إوزّة
gooseberry	'inab aθ θa'lab (m)	عنب الثعلب
grain	ḥubūb (pl)	حبوب
grape	'inab (m)	عنب
grapefruit	zinbā' (m)	زنباع

green tea	ʃāy aχḍar (m)	شاي أخضر
greens	χuḍrawāt waraqiyya (pl)	خضروات ورقيّة
halibut	samak al halbūt (m)	سمك الهلبوت
ham	hām (m)	هام
hamburger	haʃwa (f)	حشوة
hamburger	hamburger (m)	هامبورجر
hazelnut	bunduq (m)	بندق
herring	rinʒa (f)	رنجة
honey	ʿasal (m)	عسل
horseradish	fiʒl ḥārr (m)	فجل حارّ
hot	sāχin	ساخن
ice	θalʒ (m)	ثلج
ice-cream	muθallaʒāt (pl)	مثلّجات
instant coffee	niskafi (m)	نيسكافيه
jam	murabba (m)	مربّى
jam	murabba (m)	مربّى
juice	ʿaṣīr (m)	عصير
kidney bean	faṣūliya (f)	فاصوليا
kiwi	kiwi (m)	كيوي
knife	sikkīn (m)	سكّين
lamb	laḥm aḍ ḍa'n (m)	لحم الضأن
lemon	laymūn (m)	ليمون
lemonade	ʃarāb laymūn (m)	شراب ليمون
lentil	ʿadas (m)	عدس
lettuce	χass (m)	خسّ
light beer	bīra χafīfa (f)	بيرة خفيفة
liqueur	liqiūr (m)	ليكيور
liquors	maʃrūbāt kuḥūliyya (pl)	مشروبات كحوليّة
liver	kibda (f)	كبدة
lunch	ɣadā' (m)	غداء
mackerel	usqumriy (m)	أسقمريّ
mandarin	yūsufiy (m)	يوسفي
mango	mangu (m)	مانجو
margarine	marɣarīn (m)	مرغرين
marmalade	marmalād (f)	مرملاد
mashed potatoes	harīs baṭāṭis (m)	هريس بطاطس
mayonnaise	mayunīz (m)	مايونيز
meat	laḥm (m)	لحم
melon	baṭṭīχ aṣfar (f)	بطّيخ أصفر
menu	qā'imat aṭ ṭaʿām (f)	قائمة طعام
milk	ḥalīb (m)	حليب
milkshake	milk ʃyk (m)	ميلك شيك
millet	duχn (m)	دخن
mineral water	mā' maʿdaniy (m)	ماء معدنيّ
morel	fuṭr al ɣūʃna (m)	فطر الغوشنة
mushroom	fuṭr (f)	فطر
mustard	ṣalṣat al χardal (f)	صلصة الخردل
non-alcoholic	bi dūn kuḥūl	بدون كحول
noodles	nūdlis (f)	نودلز
oats	ʃūfān (m)	شوفان
olive oil	zayt az zaytūn (m)	زيت الزيتون
olives	zaytūn (m)	زيتون

omelet	bayḍ maxfūq (m)	بيض مخفوق
onion	baṣal (m)	بصل
orange	burtuqāl (m)	برتقال
orange juice	ʿaṣīr burtuqāl (m)	عصير برتقال
orange-cap boletus	fuṭr aḥmar (m)	فطر أحمر
oyster	maḥār (m)	محار
pâté	maʿʒūn laḥm (m)	معجون لحم
papaya	babāya (m)	بابايا
paprika	babrika (f)	بابريكا
parsley	baqdūnis (m)	بقدونس
pasta	makarūna (f)	مكرونة
pea	bisilla (f)	بسلّة
peach	durrāq (m)	دراق
peanut	fūl sudāniy (m)	فول سودانيّ
pear	kummaθra (f)	كمّثرى
peel	qiʃra (f)	قشرة
perch	farx (m)	فرخ
pickled	muxallil	مخلّل
pie	faṭīra (f)	فطيرة
piece	qiṭʿa (f)	قطعة
pike	samak al karāki (m)	سمك الكراكي
pike perch	samak sandar (m)	سمك سندر
pineapple	ananās (m)	أناناس
pistachios	fustuq (m)	فستق
pizza	bītza (f)	بيتزا
plate	ṭabaq (m)	طبق
plum	barqūq (m)	برقوق
poisonous mushroom	fuṭr sāmm (m)	فطر سامّ
pomegranate	rummān (m)	رمان
pork	laḥm al xinzīr (m)	لحم الخنزير
porridge	ʿaṣīda (f)	عصيدة
portion	waʒba (f)	وجبة
potato	baṭāṭis (f)	بطاطس
proteins	brutināt (pl)	بروتينات
pub, bar	bār (m)	بار
pudding	būding (m)	بودنج
pumpkin	qarʿ (m)	قرع
rabbit	arnab (m)	أرنب
radish	fiʒl (m)	فجل
raisin	zabīb (m)	زبيب
raspberry	tūt al ʿullayq al aḥmar (m)	توت العلّيق الأحمر
recipe	waṣfa (f)	وصفة
red pepper	filfil aḥmar (m)	فلفل أحمر
red wine	nabīð aḥmar (m)	نبيذ أحمر
redcurrant	kiʃmiʃ aḥmar (m)	كشمش أحمر
refreshing drink	maʃrūb muθallaʒ (m)	مشروب مثلّج
rice	urz (m)	أرز
rum	rum (m)	رم
russula	fuṭr russūla (m)	فطر روسّولا
rye	ʒāwdār (m)	جاودار
saffron	zaʿfarān (m)	زعفران
salad	sulṭa (f)	سلطة

salmon	salmūn (m)	سلمون
salt	milḥ (m)	ملح
salty	māliḥ	مالح
sandwich	sandawitʃ (m)	ساندويتش
sardine	sardīn (m)	سردين
sauce	ṣalṣa (f)	صلصة
saucer	ṭabaq finʒān (m)	طبق فنجان
sausage	suʒuq (m)	سجق
seafood	fawākih al baḥr (pl)	فواكه البحر
sesame	simsim (m)	سمسم
shark	qirʃ (m)	قرش
shrimp	ʒambari (m)	جمبري
side dish	ṭabaq ʒānibiy (m)	طبق جانبي
slice	ʃarīḥa (f)	شريحة
smoked	mudaxxin	مدخّن
soft drink	maʃrūb ɣāziy (m)	مشروب غازي
soup	ʃūrba (f)	شورية
soup spoon	mil'aqa kabīra (f)	ملعقة كبيرة
sour cream	krīma ḥāmiḍa (f)	كريمة حامضة
soy	fūl aṣ ṣūya (m)	فول الصويا
spaghetti	spaɣitti (m)	سباغيتي
sparkling	bil ɣāz	بالغاز
spice	bahār (m)	بهار
spinach	sabānix (m)	سبانخ
spiny lobster	karkand ʃāik (m)	كركند شائك
spoon	mil'aqa (f)	ملعقة
squid	kalmāri (m)	كالماري
steak	biftīk (m)	بفتيك
still	bi dūn ɣāz	بدون غاز
strawberry	farawla (f)	فراولة
sturgeon	samak al ḥaʃ (m)	سمك الحفش
sugar	sukkar (m)	سكّر
sunflower oil	zayt 'abīd aʃ ʃams (m)	زيت عبيد الشمس
sweet	musakkar	مسكّر
taste, flavor	ṭa'm (m)	طعم
tasty	laðīð	لذيذ
tea	ʃāy (m)	شاي
teaspoon	mil'aqat ʃāy (f)	ملعقة شاي
tip	baqʃīʃ (m)	بقشيش
tomato	ṭamāṭim (f)	طماطم
tomato juice	'aṣīr ṭamāṭim (m)	عصير طماطم
tongue	lisān (m)	لسان
toothpick	xallat asnān (f)	خلّة أسنان
trout	salmūn muraqqaṭ (m)	سلمون مرقّط
tuna	tūna (f)	تونة
turkey	daʒāʒ rūmiy (m)	دجاج رومي
turnip	lift (m)	لفت
veal	laḥm il 'iʒl (m)	لحم العجل
vegetable oil	zayt (m)	زيت
vegetables	xuḍār (pl)	خضار
vegetarian	nabātiy (m)	نباتي
vegetarian	nabātiy	نباتي

vermouth	virmut (m)	فيرموث
vienna sausage	suʒuq (m)	سجق
vinegar	χall (m)	خلّ
vitamin	vitamīn (m)	فيتامين
vodka	vudka (f)	فودكا
waffles	wāfil (m)	وافل
waiter	nādil (m)	نادل
waitress	nādila (f)	نادلة
walnut	'ayn al ʒamal (f)	عين الجمل
water	mā' (m)	ماء
watermelon	baṭṭīχ aḥmar (m)	بطيخ أحمر
wheat	qamḥ (m)	قمح
whiskey	wiski (m)	وسكي
white wine	nibīð abyaḍ (m)	نبيذ أبيض
wild strawberry	farāwla barriyya (f)	فراولة برّيّة
wine	nabīð (f)	نبيذ
wine list	qā'imat al χumūr (f)	قائمة خمور
with ice	biθ θalʒ	بالثلج
yogurt	yūɣurt (m)	يوغورت
zucchini	kūsa (f)	كوسة

Arabic-English gastronomic glossary

طبق فنجان	ṭabaq finʒān (m)	saucer
كبّاية	kubbāya (f)	glass
كأس	ka's (f)	glass
لحم	laḥm (m)	meat
دجاج	daʒāʒ (m)	chicken
بطّة	baṭṭa (f)	duck
إوزّة	iwazza (f)	goose
صيد	ṣayd (m)	game
دجاج رومي	daʒāʒ rūmiy (m)	turkey
لحم الخنزير	laḥm al χinzīr (m)	pork
لحم العجل	laḥm il 'iʒl (m)	veal
لحم الضأن	laḥm aḍ ḍa'n (m)	lamb
لحم البقر	laḥm al baqar (m)	beef
أرنب	arnab (m)	rabbit
سجق	suʒuq (m)	sausage
سجق	suʒuq (m)	vienna sausage
بيكون	bikūn (m)	bacon
هام	hām (m)	ham
فخذ خنزير	faχð χinzīr (m)	gammon
معجون لحم	ma'ʒūn laḥm (m)	pâté
كبدة	kibda (f)	liver
حشوة	ḥaʃwa (f)	hamburger
لسان	lisān (m)	tongue
بيضة	bayḍa (f)	egg
بيض	bayḍ (m)	eggs
بياض البيض	bayāḍ al bayḍ (m)	egg white
صفار البيض	ṣafār al bayḍ (m)	egg yolk
سمك	samak (m)	fish
فواكه البحر	fawākih al baḥr (pl)	seafood
كافيار	kaviyār (m)	caviar
سلطعون	salṭa'ūn (m)	crab
جمبري	ʒambari (m)	shrimp
محار	maḥār (m)	oyster
كركند شائك	karkand ʃāik (m)	spiny lobster
كالماري	kalmāri (m)	squid
سمك الحفش	samak al ḥafʃ (m)	sturgeon
سلمون	salmūn (m)	salmon
سمك الهلبوت	samak al halbūt (m)	halibut
سمك القدّ	samak al qudd (m)	cod
أسقمري	usqumriy (m)	mackerel
تونة	tūna (f)	tuna
حنكليس	ḥankalīs (m)	eel
سلمون مرقّط	salmūn muraqqaṭ (m)	trout
سردين	sardīn (m)	sardine

سمك الكراكي	samak al karāki (m)	pike
رنجة	rinʒa (f)	herring
خبز	χubz (m)	bread
جبنة	ʒubna (f)	cheese
سكّر	sukkar (m)	sugar
ملح	milḥ (m)	salt
أرز	urz (m)	rice
مكرونة	makarūna (f)	pasta
نودلز	nūdlis (f)	noodles
زبدة	zubda (f)	butter
زيت	zayt (m)	vegetable oil
زيت عبيد الشمس	zayt ʿabīd aʃ ʃams (m)	sunflower oil
مرغرين	marɣarīn (m)	margarine
زيتون	zaytūn (m)	olives
زيت الزيتون	zayt az zaytūn (m)	olive oil
حليب	ḥalīb (m)	milk
حليب مكثف	ḥalīb mukaθθaf (m)	condensed milk
يوغورت	yūɣurt (m)	yogurt
كريمة حامضة	krīma ḥāmiḍa (f)	sour cream
كريمة	krīma (f)	cream
مايونيز	mayunīz (m)	mayonnaise
كريمة زبدة	krīmat zubda (f)	buttercream
حبوب	ḥubūb (pl)	cereal grains
دقيق	daqīq (m)	flour
معلّبات	muʿallabāt (pl)	canned food
كورن فليكس	kurn fliks (m)	cornflakes
عسل	ʿasal (m)	honey
مربّى	murabba (m)	jam
علك	ʿilk (m)	chewing gum
ماء	māʾ (m)	water
ماء شرب	māʾ ʃurb (m)	drinking water
ماء معدنيّ	māʾ maʿdaniy (m)	mineral water
بدون غاز	bi dūn ɣāz	still
مكربن	mukarban	carbonated
بالغاز	bil ɣāz	sparkling
ثلج	θalʒ (m)	ice
بالثلج	biθ θalʒ	with ice
بدون كحول	bi dūn kuḥūl	non-alcoholic
مشروب غازي	maʃrūb ɣāziy (m)	soft drink
مشروب مثلّج	maʃrūb muθallaʒ (m)	refreshing drink
شراب ليمون	ʃarāb laymūn (m)	lemonade
مشروبات كحوليّة	maʃrūbāt kuḥūliyya (pl)	liquors
نبيذ	nabīð (f)	wine
نبيذ أبيض	nibīð abyaḍ (m)	white wine
نبيذ أحمر	nabīð aḥmar (m)	red wine
ليكيور	liqiūr (m)	liqueur
شمبانيا	ʃambāniya (f)	champagne
فيرموث	virmut (m)	vermouth
وسكي	wiski (m)	whiskey
فودكا	vudka (f)	vodka
جين	ʒīn (m)	gin
كونياك	kunyāk (m)	cognac

رم	rum (m)	rum
قهوة	qahwa (f)	coffee
قهوة سادة	qahwa sāda (f)	black coffee
قهوة بالحليب	qahwa bil ḥalīb (f)	coffee with milk
كابتشينو	kaputʃīnu (m)	cappuccino
نيسكافيه	niskafi (m)	instant coffee
كوكتيل	kuktayl (m)	cocktail
ميلك شيك	milk ʃiyk (m)	milkshake
عصير	ʿaṣīr (m)	juice
عصير طماطم	ʿaṣīr ṭamāṭim (m)	tomato juice
عصير برتقال	ʿaṣīr burtuqāl (m)	orange juice
عصير طازج	ʿaṣīr ṭāziȝ (m)	freshly squeezed juice
بيرة	bīra (f)	beer
بيرة خفيفة	bīra χafīfa (f)	light beer
بيرة غامقة	bīra ɣāmiqa (f)	dark beer
شاي	ʃāy (m)	tea
شاي أسود	ʃāy aswad (m)	black tea
شاي أخضر	ʃāy aχḍar (m)	green tea
خضار	χuḍār (pl)	vegetables
خضروات ورقيّة	χuḍrawāt waraqiyya (pl)	greens
طماطم	ṭamāṭim (f)	tomato
خيار	χiyār (m)	cucumber
جزر	ȝazar (m)	carrot
بطاطس	baṭāṭis (f)	potato
بصل	baṣal (m)	onion
ثوم	θūm (m)	garlic
كرنب	kurumb (m)	cabbage
قرنبيط	qarnabīṭ (m)	cauliflower
كرنب بروكسل	kurumb brūksil (m)	Brussels sprouts
بركولي	brukuli (m)	broccoli
بنجر	banȝar (m)	beetroot
باذنجان	bātinȝān (m)	eggplant
كوسة	kūsa (f)	zucchini
قرع	qarʿ (m)	pumpkin
لفت	lift (m)	turnip
بقدونس	baqdūnis (m)	parsley
شبت	ʃabat (m)	dill
خسّ	χass (m)	lettuce
كرفس	karafs (m)	celery
هليون	halyūn (m)	asparagus
سبانخ	sabāniχ (m)	spinach
بسلّة	bisilla (f)	pea
فول	fūl (m)	beans
ذرة	ðura (f)	corn
فاصوليا	faṣūliya (f)	kidney bean
فلفل	filfil (m)	bell pepper
فجل	fiȝl (m)	radish
خرشوف	χurʃūf (m)	artichoke
فاكهة	fākiha (f)	fruit
تفّاحة	tuffāḥa (f)	apple
كمّثرى	kummaθra (f)	pear
ليمون	laymūn (m)	lemon

برتقال	burtuqāl (m)	orange
فراولة	farawla (f)	strawberry
يوسفي	yūsufiy (m)	mandarin
برقوق	barqūq (m)	plum
دراق	durrāq (m)	peach
مشمش	miʃmiʃ (f)	apricot
توت العليق الأحمر	tūt al ʻullayq al aḥmar (m)	raspberry
أناناس	ananās (m)	pineapple
موز	mawz (m)	banana
بطّيخ أحمر	baṭṭīx aḥmar (m)	watermelon
عنب	ʻinab (m)	grape
بطّيخ أصفر	baṭṭīx aṣfar (f)	melon
زنباع	zinbāʻ (m)	grapefruit
افوكاتو	avukādu (f)	avocado
ببايا	babāya (m)	papaya
مانجو	mangu (m)	mango
رمان	rummān (m)	pomegranate
كشمش أحمر	kiʃmiʃ aḥmar (m)	redcurrant
عنب الثعلب الأسود	ʻinab aθ θaʻlab al aswad (m)	blackcurrant
عنب الثعلب	ʻinab aθ θaʻlab (m)	gooseberry
عنب الأحراج	ʻinab al aḥrāʒ (m)	bilberry
ثمر العليّق	θamar al ʻullayk (m)	blackberry
زبيب	zabīb (m)	raisin
تين	tīn (m)	fig
تمر	tamr (m)	date
فول سوداني	fūl sudāniy (m)	peanut
لوز	lawz (m)	almond
عين الجمل	ʻayn al ʒamal (f)	walnut
بندق	bunduq (m)	hazelnut
جوز هند	ʒawz al hind (m)	coconut
فستق	fustuq (m)	pistachios
حلويّات	ḥalawiyyāt (pl)	confectionery
بسكويت	baskawīt (m)	cookies
شكولاتة	ʃukulāta (f)	chocolate
بالشكولاتة	biʃ ʃukulāṭa	chocolate
بونبون	bumbūn (m)	candy
كعك	kaʻk (m)	cake
تورتة	tūrta (f)	cake
فطيرة	faṭīra (f)	pie
حشوة	ḥaʃwa (f)	filling
مربّى	murabba (m)	jam
مرملاد	marmalād (f)	marmalade
وافل	wāfil (m)	waffles
مثلّجات	muθallaʒāt (pl)	ice-cream
وجبة	waʒba (f)	course, dish
مطبخ	matbax (m)	cuisine
وصفة	waṣfa (f)	recipe
وجبة	waʒba (f)	portion
سلطة	sulṭa (f)	salad
شورية	ʃūrba (f)	soup
مرق	maraq (m)	clear soup

ساندويتش	sandawitʃ (m)	sandwich
بيض مقليّ	bayḍ maqliy (m)	fried eggs
هامبورجر	hamburger (m)	hamburger
بفتيك	biftīk (m)	steak
طبق جانبيّ	ṭabaq ӡānibiy (m)	side dish
سباغيتي	spaɣitti (m)	spaghetti
هريس بطاطس	harīs baṭāṭis (m)	mashed potatoes
بيتزا	bītza (f)	pizza
عصيدة	‘aṣīda (f)	porridge
بيض مخفوق	bayḍ maxfūq (m)	omelet
مسلوق	maslūq	boiled
مدخّن	mudaxxin	smoked
مقليّ	maqliy	fried
مجفّف	muӡaffaf	dried
مجمّد	muӡammad	frozen
مخلّل	muxallil	pickled
مسكّر	musakkar	sweet
مالح	māliḥ	salty
بارد	bārid	cold
ساخن	sāxin	hot
مرّ	murr	bitter
لذيذ	laðīð	tasty
قشرة	qiʃra (f)	peel
فلفل أسود	filfil aswad (m)	black pepper
فلفل أحمر	filfil aḥmar (m)	red pepper
صلصة الخردل	ṣalṣat al xardal (f)	mustard
فجل حارّ	fiӡl ḥārr (m)	horseradish
تابل	tābil (m)	condiment
بهار	bahār (m)	spice
صلصة	ṣalṣa (f)	sauce
خلّ	xall (m)	vinegar
يانسون	yānsūn (m)	anise
ريحان	rīḥān (m)	basil
قرنفل	qurumful (m)	cloves
زنجبيل	zanӡabīl (m)	ginger
كزبرة	kuzbara (f)	coriander
قرفة	qirfa (f)	cinnamon
سمسم	simsim (m)	sesame
أوراق الغار	awrāq al ɣār (pl)	bay leaf
بابريكا	babrika (f)	paprika
كراوية	karāwiya (f)	caraway
زعفران	za‘farān (m)	saffron
أكل	akl (m)	food
فطور	fuṭūr (m)	breakfast
غداء	ɣadā’ (m)	lunch
عشاء	‘aʃā’ (m)	dinner
شهيّة	ʃahiyya (f)	appetite
إهنيئًا مريئًا!	hanī’an marī’an!	Enjoy your meal!
طعم	ṭa‘m (m)	taste, flavor
المذاق العالق في الفم	al maðāq al ‘āliq fil fam (m)	aftertaste
حمية غذائية	ḥimya ɣaðā’iyya (f)	diet
فيتامين	vitamīn (m)	vitamin

سعرة حرارية	su'ra ḥarāriyya (f)	calorie
نباتيّ	nabātiy (m)	vegetarian
نباتيّ	nabātiy	vegetarian
دهون	duhūn (pl)	fats
بروتينات	brutināt (pl)	proteins
نشويّات	naʃawiyyāt (pl)	carbohydrates
شريحة	ʃarīḥa (f)	slice
قطعة	qiṭ'a (f)	piece
فتاتة	futāta (f)	crumb
ملعقة	mil'aqa (f)	spoon
سكّين	sikkīn (m)	knife
شوكة	ʃawka (f)	fork
فنجان	finʒān (m)	cup
طبق	ṭabaq (m)	plate
خلّة أسنان	xallat asnān (f)	toothpick
بار	bār (m)	pub, bar
نادل	nādil (m)	waiter
نادلة	nādila (f)	waitress
بارمان	bārman (m)	bartender
قائمة طعام	qā'imat aṭ ṭa'ām (f)	menu
قائمة خمور	qā'imat al xumūr (f)	wine list
شراب	ʃarāb (m)	aperitif
مقبّلات	muqabbilāt (pl)	appetizer
حلويّات	ḥalawiyyāt (pl)	dessert
حساب	ḥisāb (m)	check
بقشيش	baqʃīʃ (m)	tip
ملعقة شاي	mil'aqat ʃāy (f)	teaspoon
ملعقة كبيرة	mil'aqa kabīra (f)	soup spoon
فتّاحة	fattāḥa (f)	bottle opener
فتّاحة	fattāḥa (f)	can opener
بريمة	barrīma (f)	corkscrew
أبراميس	abramīs (m)	bream
شبّوط	ʃabbūṭ (m)	carp
فرخ	farx (m)	perch
قرموط	qarmūṭ (m)	catfish
سلمون أطلسيّ	salmūn aṭlasiy (m)	Atlantic salmon
سمك مفلطح	samak mufalṭaḥ (m)	flatfish
سمك سندر	samak sandar (m)	pike perch
قرش	qirʃ (m)	shark
فطر	fuṭr (f)	mushroom
فطر صالح للأكل	fuṭr ṣāliḥ lil akl (m)	edible mushroom
فطر سامّ	fuṭr sāmm (m)	poisonous mushroom
فطر بوليط مأكول	fuṭr bulīṭ ma'kūl (m)	cep
فطر أحمر	fuṭr aḥmar (m)	orange-cap boletus
فطر بوليط	fuṭr bulīṭ (m)	birch bolete
فطر كويزي	fuṭr kwīzi (m)	chanterelle
فطر روسّولا	fuṭr russūla (m)	russula
فطر الغوشنة	fuṭr al ɣūʃna (m)	morel
فطر أمانيت الطائر السامّ	fuṭr amānīt aṭ ṭā'ir as sāmm (m)	fly agaric
فطر أمانيت فالوسياني السامّ	fuṭr amānīt falusyāniy as sāmm (m)	death cap

توت أحمر برّيّ	tūt aḥmar barriy (m)	cranberry
كيوي	kiwi (m)	kiwi
حبّة	ḥabba (f)	berry
حبّات	ḥabbāt (pl)	berries
عنب الثور	'inab aθ θawr (m)	cowberry
فراولة برّيّة	farāwla barriyya (f)	wild strawberry
حبوب	ḥubūb (pl)	grain
محاصيل الحبوب	maḥāṣīl al ḥubūb (pl)	cereal crops
سنبلة	sumbula (f)	ear
قمح	qamḥ (m)	wheat
جاودار	ʒāwdār (m)	rye
شوفان	ʃūfān (m)	oats
دخن	duxn (m)	millet
شعير	ʃaʿīr (m)	barley
ذرة	ðura (f)	corn
حنطة سوداء	ḥinṭa sawdā' (f)	buckwheat
فول الصويا	fūl aṣ ṣūya (m)	soy
عدس	'adas (m)	lentil
بودنج	būding (m)	pudding
ثمر	θamr (m)	fruits